Enneagram

A Complete Guide to the Search for Harmony

Vince Oliver

Table of Contents

Introduction

"Who am I? Why do these things keep happening to me? Why do I feel this way? What is my purpose and role in this world? How can I be better, happier? Why do my relationships challenge me so much? Is this normal? Why can't I get through to my kids, my coworkers? Why am I so unhappy and demotivated at work?"

These, and many other questions, pass through our minds daily.

Looking at Megan – the healthy glow in her cheeks and confident smile, the air of peace and calm she exuded, it was difficult to imagine that a few short months before that she had been in full breakdown mode, suffering angina and panic attacks and battling with severe depression and anxiety.

"I had been in a high-powered corporate job in quality management for over 20 years," Megan related. "It was complicated, involving intense knowledge of intricate legalese and my life was a continual battle trying to get the 'creatives' in our group to understand and apply the rules so that our company didn't fail quality audits and basically get shut down."

"Honestly, I hated the work. It was painfully dull, and I was stuck in the position of always playing 'bad cop' with the rest of the team, as I was the one who had to communicate often nonsensical red-tape requirements to them. I pretty much know that they laughed at me behind my back and called me 'The Queen Bee' because they believed I was so bossy, pedantic, and nitpicking.

But I could do it well, understand and apply the systems in such a way that it made them as user-friendly as possible for my team. I did my best to get us through all the audits, but with the growing and changing business, combined with people's inability to understand how important it was to follow the legislated requirements, the monthly official reviews became a nightmare for me. These external bodies doing the checks could literally shut us down, depending on what they found.

When the workplace changed management and communication broke down between departments – the toxicity grew unbearable.

For weeks I found myself coming home and just lying on the couch staring at the wall. I didn't even have the words to describe how bad I felt."

The pain and discomfort – and, in fact, full break down and burnout she was experiencing was a springboard to a whole new way of life for her and her family.

"Understanding my Enneatype made a huge difference. A lot fell into place for me then. Mainly the reasons why I was so stressed and miserable in my job.

I realized I needed to make a difference in the world. I realized that I needed to rise above my need for stability and take a few risks, and I also saw how who I was being was in part, to blame for the situation I found myself in."

Megan walked out of that toxic environment after 23 years of devoted labor and didn't look back. She has now started her own coaching business, where her love of psychology and human growth feeds her soul. She finds the time to get out of doors and into nature, spend time with her two sons, and to focus on her own studies.

It's like looking at a whole new person. Her inner peace shines through her face like a light.

"It was the self-awareness and understanding of who I was and what I needed to do to take myself to the next level, that made all the difference. I was able to leave behind a way of being and set of choices that weren't working for my work team, my family, my career, or my soul."

Megan is not alone in a story like this. There are so many of us sitting in discomfort, struggling to find meaning, to handle our stress, and hoping for happiness, which sometimes seems out of our grasp, no matter what we do.

For sure, some of us seem to have it together a bit better than others. But none of us are perfect. We all have moments of doubt about life, work, ourselves, our loved ones, and our place in this world.

Only with the awareness of self and others can we really understand what we need to do to shift and improve our lives.

This book answers these questions and more, giving you a simple, practical, and easy-to-use guide to a personality theory that has become world-famous for its fun practicality and applicability to our everyday lives.

Chapter 1: The Enneagram - What Is It and How Can It Help Me?

Happiness is something we all want. We go through life trying one thing after another in the search for it. And yet, so many of us never quite seem to get there.

Why?

We believe that happiness and success is something we can only find out there, somewhere external to ourselves. Media and society teach a misplaced lesson to us, from an early age, that if only we can get those new shoes, that better job, this new car, or that perfect soulmate, we will achieve the ideal state of bliss.

And we reach out and grab for it - only to find that when we have that new car, new partner or promotion, that we feel no different. Our expectations are dashed and disappointed. Some of us think, "Oh well, maybe I wanted the wrong thing, or chose the wrong person." We try again - with a new idea, thing, or partner, in search of a holy grail.

There is a growing consciousness that we need to look beyond external things or achievements. Humanity begins to understand what many enlightened gurus have been trying to tell us for centuries.

Happiness is an inside job. And to understand how to find it - we must start with self-awareness.

Only by knowing what is going on inside our heads, hearts, and souls will we find the true path to happiness and inner peace.

Studying the Enneagram not only helps you understand yourself more - allowing you to better manage thoughts, feelings, and life choices, but it also helps you understand others from their own perspective too.

Living on Autopilot

There are so many things to do - lessons to learn, certificates, and qualifications to be achieved, partners to be found, families to be started, not to mention the humdrum of functional life. If you wrote down your list of all you do - from the laundry, shopping, and cooking dinner to managing everyone's health, happiness, and growth in your home - it could seem overwhelmingly long. Just thinking about it is exhausting!

It is so easy to get caught up in a functional life - ruled by our to-do lists. There always seems like there is so much to do.

We can end up in a sort of hibernation - or zombie-like state - moving through our lives from task to task - just trying to survive and get through the day. And sometimes that's ok. Sometimes - like when you have a new baby in the house, or you are studying for exams - you literally just need to get through what is required, and time for more self-actualizing activities is set aside.

This is fine for short periods. But not forever.

The problem is that once we are in that state, we may not even realize it. Our lives unfold on "automatic" - a bit like that movie *Click*, with Adam Sandler. In the movie, he fast-forwarded whole sections of his life without genuinely experiencing them, enjoying them, or really learning anything. He fast-forwarded through marital arguments, exhausting childcare, and rushed ahead to work promotions and success until the end when he realized he had missed it all.

Unconscious Patterns and Strategies

From before birth and throughout our lives, we are learning. What we learn depends on so many variable factors. From what we hear, what we are told and taught, what we see others doing, what we read and watch in the media to ideas we come up with on our own.

What we don't always realize is that everybody has a different set of input - we may have some things in common - for example, in a shared culture, we may all learn that a particular behavior is acceptable or not. But what we ultimately learn and 'know' is cobbled together from a relatively unique set of experiences.

Each one of us learns ways of surviving and interacting with this world, based on what we have learned.

The way an only child, growing up in an abusive, single-parent home with a narcissistic mother has learned to be, will be vastly different from what another person growing up in a warm, stable, nurturing environment surrounded by a supportive family has learned about the world.

These experiences will determine what they think the world is and how they interact with it.

And most of us aren't even aware of this. We don't realize how we have been programmed or that others are programmed differently. We live according to a set of knowledge, rules, and habits which sometimes work and sometimes really don't. And while we may be disappointed when our programs and patterns don't work, we don't really understand why things didn't go as planned. Next time a challenge arises, we will revert to a similar pattern of behavior. Only to be disappointed yet again.

"The definition of insanity is doing the same thing, again and again, and expecting a different result." - Einstein.

So, how do we get a different result?

How do we shift our lives away from unhelpful choices and interactions - and move towards happiness, peace, stability, and real and supportive relationships with others?

A Light Turns On

If we are lucky, with experience and age, we begin to understand a little bit more about ourselves. If we are fortunate and wise, we eventually realize that we need to stop and look at our thoughts, behavior patterns, and choices.

It can take a loss, a great deal of discomfort, or a change to jolt us into this realization. But if we can get past the pain of bad experiences and use them to learn, we begin to awaken.

We see that we are not achieving the results we want. We move from unconscious habits and patterns towards a more conscious observation of the self.

Only in this way have we got any hope of changing ourselves and our lives for the better.

The Enneagram of Personality is a popular way to achieve the self-awareness and understanding we need to grow and succeed in all spheres of life.

The journey of really unpacking how the Enneagram works and applying it to your life and relationships, provide you with a way to see things differently, and recognizing and changing old, unconscious patterns of behavior.

It gives you a chance to try something new to get different, and hopefully, better results.

Wouldn't Einstein be proud of us?

The Purpose of the Enneagram

As your understanding and self-awareness grow, it can feel like an awakening. Suddenly you see the world more clearly. And, with clarity and understanding, comes immense freedom.

You are no longer stuck on mindless repeat and replay.

"When I discover who I am, I'll be free." – Ralph Ellison

You now have the choice between old, unhelpful patterns and new, potentially life-changing decisions which can make all the difference to you.

Using the Enneagram model, you will be able to get a better picture of who you are, and your possible strengths and weaknesses. It will help you recognize unhealthy patterns of behavior, which may be causing hardships and difficulties for you and show the way to work through them for healthier future choices.

Investigating your Enneagram personality type is a practical and powerful way to achieve the self-knowledge we need to make any kind of positive change.

The Enneagram will work for you if:

1. You are the kind of person who loves learning about yourself, always seeking ways for greater understanding and improvement.
2. You want better relationships at home, work, or just in general.

3. You want to be a better parent and raise happy, competent children.
4. You like to understand others - what makes them tick and how to relate and communicate better with them.
5. You are a manager or team leader and want to understand your team - learn how to motivate and manage them for optimal performance.
6. You are a therapist, counselor, or similar and want to broaden your knowledge of personality types and contribute more to your clients' development.
7. You are in the business world and want to improve productivity, sales, and customer relations.

And if none of that convinces you, ask yourself one simple question, "Has what I know about myself and others, really been working for me until now?"

If you have any doubt - a little more information cannot hurt.

What is the Enneagram?

The Enneagram model comes from ancient teachings, which have been refined by psychologists and scientists in recent years and become widely used and popular as a personality categorization theory.

In Greek, ennea means nine, and gramma means letters or characters. (from the Greek words ἐννέα [ennéa, meaning "nine"] and γράμμα [gramma, meaning "written" or "drawn").

It looks a bit like a weird kind of occult symbol - but in fact, it has an easily explained scientific base.

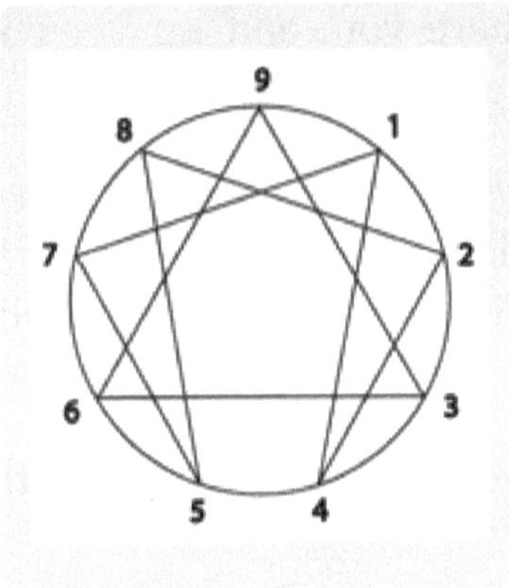

The nine numbers you see on the diagram stand for the nine personality types - which we will discuss more in Chapter 2.

"Only nine types?" you say. "Surely, there are more than nine types of people in the world?"

And you would be right.

The main idea is that each main type sees the world differently and has different underlying motivations that affect how we think, feel, and behave.

The Enneagram model, you will find, is also super flexible and, while using the nine main categories, supports category shift depending on the situation and type of stress a person is under. Although your main category dominates most of your actions throughout your life - the Enneagram also explains how we can experience and manifest the patterns of other personality types in different situations.

In the Enneagram, each type is connected with 2 other types by arrows - which show a *Stress Point* and a direction pointing towards a comfort state. The "comfort state" is that state of being where a person is stable, happy, and not under stress.

A stress point is where you 'end up' if you are imbalanced or under pressure over a more extended period of time.

There are also *Triads* - each containing three of the Enneagram categories, which align to a main subset of thinking, feeling, or action. And *Wings*, which are the neighboring numbers to each category.

This allows for a lot of individuality within the framework of the theory.

It sounds like a lot of numbers and things to remember - especially if you're not a numbers person. But don't despair - it's going to get much clearer and easier to understand as we go along.

If you wanted a map to the buried treasure, this is it. Except the treasure is worth so much more than just gold. It is success and growth in every area of your life.

Are you ready to start the treasure trail?

Chapter 2: The Nine Personality Types

Part 1

Let's start with the basics, the nine different Enneatypes. In Chapter 9, we provide a few tests to help you determine your type and that of those around you. For now, see if you can recognize yourself or others you know well in one of the main types.

A side note - in each type, we have given a case study - and often, these are quite extreme cases. Even the best, most self-aware parents are going to be raising one Enneatype child or another, and it is relatively impossible to find a perfect path. You cannot raise a child in a glass jar, surrounded by cotton wool, fairies, and unicorns. And even that would be wrong.

Only struggle and imperfection grow us as human beings.

Sometimes we have had tough childhoods - and carry the scars many years later. What is essential to understand is that no-one is perfect - and parents generally do their best with the knowledge they have at the time.

When we can recognize our own type, and those around us, we can identify how to shift towards harmony with our inner selves and our outer worlds. With the knowledge comes understanding, and perhaps forgiveness and healing for all.

Enneatype 1 *- The Reformer/Perfectionist*

"Every block of stone has a statue inside it, and it is the task of he sculptor to discover it." - Michelangelo.

"So, the pie isn't perfect? Cut it into wedges. Stay in control, and never panic." – Martha Stewart.

Type ones just really want to be good, and they want to help make the world a better place too. They tend to be rational, principled, and judgmental, with a strong desire for justice, equality, and fairness. They have a strong sense of right and wrong.

Core Value: Perfection. Doing your best and living up to your potential, being accurate, virtuous, and right.

When Jenny remembers her childhood, she has quite a hard tale to tell.

"When my grandma died, my mom said, 'Now you will be the one who is strong for me,'" she remembers.

"Even though I wasn't the eldest, I was the eldest girl and was made responsible for all the other children in the house, including my older brother, who got away with everything. I was the one who had to keep order, keep the place clean, make the food, and make sure the younger ones were safe, behaved, and did their homework. I was only about 9 when all this responsibility was handed to me. I really don't remember having much of a childhood at all."

Even before she became the nominal mother in her family, little Jenny had had to face a tough road with her mother, who showed strong narcissistic tendencies, and had made Jenny her Golden Child. She was always told how good and smart she was, while at the same time told she would never be as clever as her brother. They were not allowed to freely express, and the phrase, 'children should be seen and not heard,' was often used in her home. Any extremes of emotion - even laughing - were expressly forbidden and harshly punished.

Not every type One has such an abusive childhood - but whatever has happened, they have learned that being good and perfect is rewarded, and anything else is unacceptable. They often have to be the 'heroes' of the show - playing parent or caregiver or a perfect child. They thought if they could just get it right, everything would be ok.

So, you can understand why being good - as a person and at any task - is so very important to a One. It is literally core to their survival - as they have learned from a very young age.

Jenny is aware now of how her childhood has shaped her, and while she is frustrated at how it made her so rigid and judgmental, she is using the Enneagram to help her understand and question her less helpful tendencies.

Core Fear: Being wrong, bad, unacceptable, inappropriate, unteachable, corrupted, or out of control.

Core Weakness: Ones can become very angry and resentful. Anger can turn into depression.

Maladaptive behavior: At their worst, Ones will be obsessed with an idealized self-image. Deep down, they believe they are not good enough, and to keep themselves safe from criticism, they hold unrealistically high standards. They can't take criticism - it is integral to survival to be perfect, so they will lash out reactively. They need to be right and fear being wrong in any way.

They try to be perfect and do most things perfectly in order to be acceptable to others and to themselves.

There is a frequent disconnect between the world as it is, and what they think it should be. They resent the fact that it is not a perfect world. Reality will always fall short, and they will always be in resistance and angry about it.

They can be quite self-righteous and vengeful.

They are angry, but they face a perpetual inner struggle around it because they have also been taught that good children shouldn't be angry. So, they either deny their anger or repress it - often leading to depression.

They often project their high standards onto others - although not as harshly as they measure themselves.

They can be scary, angry, hard people. Nothing is right or as it should be, and they are going to make themselves and everyone around them pay. They resent that the world doesn't recognize their efforts.

They tense their jaws and clench their teeth, pushing through regardless. They must make things perfect right now. It's a challenge for Ones to leave things alone and just let them be.

Core Strengths: Good at creating and following rules and structure, and highly principled, Ones are also conscientious, dedicated, persevering, reliable, hard-working, and industrious. They are great at seeing and fixing details. They intuitively compare the present reality to its ideal state, know what is missing and what should be there. They are all about fairness, accuracy, and order.

At their best, they can be great leaders, planners, and systems-thinkers. They are great advocates for justice and fairness. They are rational, balanced, and chase knowledge and wisdom.

Adaptive behavior: When a One is in harmony with self, they realize that perfection is an unfolding process - and work continually on themselves without too much judgement. They know that they are moving towards completion and wholeness, and that's ok.

They are serene, at ease with themselves, relaxed and mindful. They know when to act and when to let go.

Key Developmental Areas:

1. Expressing emotions, especially anger, in safe ways.
2. Managing expectations and anger.
3. Learning to let go and let be.
4. Relaxing - learning to meditate and release all the effort, and to let life naturally unfold at its own pace.
5. Play and have fun.
6. Self-acceptance and acceptance of what is versus what they think things should be. It's ok to not be perfect.
7. Flow mentality.
8. Recognizing the beauty in imperfection.
9. Trying to understand gray areas in life.
10. "I am therefore I am good," replaces "I have to be perfect to be acceptable."

Possible Careers: Anything with clear parameters and consistency, supporting justice, fairness, good ethics, and what they believe to be right.

They do well in quality control, management, the law, social leadership, social work/guidance, medicine, journalism, accounting, planning, and project-management.

Physical Signs of Type One:

1. A perfect and beautiful home. And also, sometimes a train-wreck because they haven't had the time to make it perfect that day.
2. A tidy desk or an explosion of paper. If it's messy, they will silently seethe and be outwardly grumpy.
3. Lots of to-do lists - they love lists and PowerPoint.
4. They have planned next Christmas already, and it's only Valentine's Day.
5. That person who likes to be helpful and tell you what you're doing wrong.
6. Perfectionists.
7. Neatly groomed and clean and tidy.
8. Always on time - or a little early.
9. Owns a label-maker, and maybe even a laminator too.
10. Shrugs off compliments but seethes about one possible criticism for days or longer.
11. Battles to sleep - lies awake worrying.
12. Corrects your spelling and grammar.
13. Stubborn.
14. Great at giving an honest opinion - even when you don't ask for one.
15. Gets road rage against anyone not completely obeying all the traffic rules.
16. Loves reading self-improvement books.

Famous Type Ones: Margaret Thatcher, Steve Jobs, Julie Andrews, CS Lewis, Mahatma Gandhi, Rudy Giuliani.

What TV Characters Match this Type?

Miranda Hobbes from *Sex and the City*.

Hermione Granger in *Harry Potter*.

Enneatype 2 - The Caregiver

"I love the fact that I can make people happy in any form. Even if it's just an hour of their lives, if I can make them feel lucky or make them feel good, or bring a smile to a sour face, that to me is worthwhile."
- Freddie Mercury

Type Twos wants to be fully loved, accepted and wanted. They are supportive advisors, generous, demonstrative, people-pleasing, and sometimes possessive.

Core Value: Being appreciated, loved, and wanted.

Karen is a typical Two. Growing up, she was rewarded for helping and giving. "I had to be cute, funny, and charming if I wanted my parents' attention," she says.

"So long as I pleased them, fetched their drinks, did my chores, didn't talk back or upset their world in any way, I was petted and fussed over. The minute I didn't behave like a perfect little robot, I was sent out of the room and often punished for being unruly."

Karen was never really allowed just to be herself, to be a normal kid. She was expected to be some kind of super child - the child every other parent would envy. This meant normal expression and needs were quickly squashed down, and it became all about pleasing others to survive.

Twos learn that they are not important unless they are helpful, obliging, and pleasing, that they will only be loved if they do what others want or need, and are seen doing so.

Core Fear: Twos fear rejection. They get their validation from how others see them. Their self-worth depends on other people's opinions of them, not in themselves. They do not want to be seen as needy because that would not be pleasing or acceptable.

Their worst fear is being thought worthless, as then they will be unworthy of love and cast aside.

They have been taught that to be accepted and included, they must do what pleases others and because we are social animals - rejection is truly an instinctive danger.

Core Weakness: Twos can be a bit of a martyr. They even take pride in how much they give and can force help on people who haven't even asked for it.

Maladaptive behavior: They give help to be accepted and to make people feel grateful and like them, rather than giving help from a position of strength, choice, and true free will.

They take pride in how helpful they can be - even when that help isn't wanted or turns sour. And they think if they show others what love looks like - then others will give that same love back to them. They keep hoping others will do unto them as they do unto others. They believe only after helping others will they be helped.

They may not accept help easily - having pride in being the helper and not the helped.

They want everybody to need them, and they want to be important in people's lives. They believe that what they do for others is the only way to get love. They give so they can get.

They are compulsive helpers and rescuers. They can be seen as overbearing sometimes.

Twos can feel resentful when others make no effort to meet their unspoken needs. When their expectations of returned service aren't met, they get angry and upset. They play the martyr and the victim. They can lose touch with their own compassion and become tough, bitter, and cynical in a reaction to the situation.

They might even want to get even with people for not returning their love and care.

And yet they are often not even aware of what their own needs are - as these are avoided or squashed down.

They take pride in what great helpers they are - and can burn out because they do not have unlimited resources.

Core Strengths: Twos have super spider-senses when it comes to seeing the needs of others because they have developed this as a survival tool. They are intuitive, empathetic, and compassionate.

Adaptive Behavior: They can be humble, giving, warm, and kind. They have learned to say no and set boundaries. They have worked on their self-worth so that they understand love cannot be controlled and is freely given and received.

They are sociable, likable, friendly, and approachable. They are good with praise, boosting and motivating others, and make great listeners and counselors. They often support the weak and underprivileged underdog.

They feel fulfilled in giving but have learned to communicate expectations and their own needs, and take joy from the act of giving itself without needing anything in return.

Key Developmental Areas:

1. Expressing expectations.
2. Internalizing self-worth based on self and not others.
3. Self-care.
4. Asking for and accepting help.

5. Identifying what is important to them and what they need.
6. Looking to self to fulfill needs.
7. Creating boundaries.
8. Facing, understanding, and accepting their shadow side.
9. "I am therefore I am worthy" replaces "I have to give to be loved."

Possible careers: Anything where they can make new friends and help others. They want strong working relationships and enjoy service. Non-profits, religious careers, human resources, nursing, counselors, teachers, humanitarians, and customer service careers all work well for this type.

Physical Signs of Type Two:

1. They struggle to say no.
2. They are great hosts - taking care of your every need before you even know you have one.
3. They love recognition and quietly glow when you praise them.
4. People always go to them with their problems.
5. They love to listen.
6. They will be the one washing the dishes after a party.
7. Can be prickly when you offer to help.
8. They remember your birthday, all the stuff you told them about 3rd grade, and what your favorite perfume is.
9. They are the ones to ask if you need to know about anyone's personal life.

Famous Type Twos: Mother Teresa, Nancy Reagan, Debbie Reynolds, Lewis Carrol, Stevie Wonder.

What TV Characters Match this Type?

Jane Villanueva from *Jane the Virgin*.

Molly Weasley in *Harry Potter*.

Enneatype 3 - The Achiever

"Don't be upset by the results you didn't get with the work you didn't do."
– Steven Antoine.

"Find your light. They can't love you if they can't see you."
– Bette Midler.

Type Three must succeed and achieve. They are effective, adaptable, driven, and image conscious.

Core Value: They want to be valued and accepted. They value efficiency.

Ken was that little boy who always got all the certificates at the school assembly. "I used to get paid by my parents for getting A's," he remembers. "My dad really wanted me to excel at sports, attending all my games, and cheering from the sidelines. But I always felt my achievements were somehow actually his, and if we lost a game, or I did badly at school, he would barely speak to me for days."

"My little brother wasn't as good at sports and school studies, and my dad had barely any time for him. I got all the treats and attention when I did well."

A type Three is usually raised to believe their achievements are everything - and performance and image are rewarded over being vulnerable or forming real human connections.

They must be something super-special to be recognized and valued, and that is always way more than just being themselves. They crave respect and admiration. This represents what love is for a Three.

Core Fear: A Three fears being seen as incompetent, worthless, or a failure, because then they believe they will be worth nothing.

They have been taught that to be accepted and included, they must always be achieving.

Core Weakness: They can be deceptive - painting an image of success that isn't real. They put a lot of effort into presenting a perfect, polished exterior to the world. They play a character instead of being themselves.

Maladaptive behavior: Success at all costs carries a high price that Threes don't want to acknowledge. Deep down, they believe they are failures and that everything they do is an act. Soon they may be exposed if they don't keep the act seamless, and they work hard to fill in the gaps. They can and do burn out.

They won't take on projects if they think they can't shine in them.

Impostor syndrome is a thing. To compensate, they become overly efficient and too image conscious. They cannot always be believed; they are all about the sizzle and little to do with the steak.

They can become workaholics - investing their self-worth entirely on climbing the ladder of success. The end justifies the means.

They have great difficulty accepting or even considering failure. They lose touch with what they want, who they are, and what they really feel.

Core Strengths: Charismatic, confident, productive, adaptable, and efficient. They have great organizational skills, work well towards goals, and are very self-motivated. They know what looks good and how to present themselves and their ideas. They can sense what others want and fit in with them easily. They connect well with others.

Adaptive Behavior: At their best, they know that chaos won't erupt the minute they take time off. They know that the best way is to walk in the truth, be vulnerable and authentic and true to themselves too. They understand that they are human beings, not human doings.

They are clear on their values and stick with them regardless of what others do or say. They cooperate rather than compete and embrace failure as a natural part of learning and growth.

They can relax and accept that their value is not attached to what they do or how others perceive them.

Key Developmental Areas:

1. Acknowledging the masks, they wear to fit in and please others.
2. Finding value in self, not just accomplishments.
3. Gratitude for what they have.
4. Getting to know who they really are.
5. Being vulnerable - and realizing the strength in that.
6. Focusing on self rather than others.
7. Accepting there is enough for everyone - no one has to win or lose.
8. "I am, therefore, I am worthy" replaces "I have to give to be loved."

Possible Careers: Entrepreneur, politician, marketing or advertising executive, lawyer, or salesperson.

Physical Signs of Type Three:

1. Always smiling.
2. Kisses babies.
3. Tries to connect.
4. Wears the best workout gear at the gym.
5. Drives a great car and lives in a good neighborhood.

6. Loves holding dinner parties and functions.
7. Has lots of certificates, trophies, and awards on their shelf.

Famous Type Threes: Lady Gaga, Justin Bieber, Will Smith, Oprah Winfrey.

What TV Characters Match this Type?

Veronica Lodge from *Riverdale*.

Gilderoy Lockhart in *Harry Potter*

Enneatype 4 - The Individualist/Creative

"Always be a first-rate version of yourself instead of a second-rate'
– Judy Garland.

Type Fours are expressive, dramatic, self-absorbed, and temperamental. They really want to be special.

Core Value: Beauty, originality, authenticity, and uniqueness are key to these individuals. Anything that supports real expression, the inner journey, as well as the outer journey of connection to others.

Jenny grew up mostly alone. Her extremely gifted parents were seldom home, each pursuing a career and a passion of their own. Her father was a scientist and her mother, an opera singer.

"I had nannies and people around all the time, but all I wanted was my parents' attention. I believed I had to follow in their footsteps in order to be included in their world. I believed we were a special family, and I had to get them to see me as gifted as they were so that I wouldn't be left behind."

Jenny didn't have her mother's talent for music, but she pushed herself to become one of the most lauded neurosurgeons of her time. Even then, she admits, she never really felt like she belonged to her family or anywhere else. "I always imagined that my real parents, maybe some sort of royalty or something even better than my actual mom and dad, would come to get me," she says.

Fours learn that they need to be above and beyond, gifted, special, different from the rest, in order to be noticed.

Core Fear: Being ordinary, average, and boring. Not mattering or being inadequate and insignificant.

They have learned that to be accepted and included, they must be special.

Core Weakness: Fours can be overly sensitive and focused on the image they are projecting to the world. Deep down, they feel something is wrong with them compared to others, and only by being special will they find acceptance.

They believe they need to make an impression to be remembered.

They need attention, and they need to be better and different enough to keep that attention.

Maladaptive behavior: Fours will go out of their way to be, or appear to be, special. They must be the highest leaper in ballet, the bendiest at yoga, the most genius at science, the most skilled in their field - whatever it is they choose.

They constantly compare themselves to others and come up short in their own minds.

Envy consumes them, loneliness, and melancholy highlight them. By seeking to stand out from the pack, they rarely feel part of it. How can they ever feel "normal?"

Drama and fantasy - their made-up world where they are all they need to be - can overtake reality. They are moody, tragically misunderstood, and disconnected. Fearing abandonment, they often push away anybody they could connect with, creating the very thing they fear in a sad, self-fulfilling prophecy.

Core Strengths: Sensitive, refined, and connected to self and others. Fours have a strong intuition, imagination, and sense of what is aesthetically pleasing. They can make the ordinary, extraordinary.

Adaptive Behavior: Once a Four realizes that they are already unique - just like everybody else - and worthy, they can relax and enjoy what they have already achieved.

Finding inner and outer balance and fulfillment as they are - they can be in harmony in the present moment. They can let go of the drama and just be happy and at peace at the moment.

They know they can be seen and loved for exactly who they are - special and unique as is.

Key Developmental Areas:

1. Realize that they are good enough as they are.
2. Gain self-worth based on inner qualities rather than on skills.
3. Being authentic and vulnerable.
4. Getting perspective - taking time to walk in another's shoes.
5. Gratitude for what they have versus what they don't.
6. Recognizing self-centered thoughts.
7. Using breath work to stay calm.
8. Practicing mindfulness.
9. Allowing space for people to connect be letting others into their world.
10. "I am, therefore I am unique." replaces "I have to be special to be loved."

Possible Careers: Actor, writer, artist, designer, dancer, photographer. Anything that lets them be autonomous and shine.

Physical Signs of Type Four:

1. Sitting alone at a party.
2. Drama Queen/King.
3. Can't keep a relationship for long.

4. Very up and down emotionally.
5. Disappears when stressed.
6. Gets stressed when criticized.
7. Loves talking about feelings.
8. Blossoms when someone shows a genuine interest in them.
9. Hates being interrupted.

Famous Type Fours: Sylvia Plath, Kate Winslet, Gene Wilder, Edgar Allen Poe, Amy Winehouse, Taylor Swift.

What TV Characters Match this Type?

Phoebe Buffay in *Friends*

Luna Lovegood in *Harry Potter*

Enneatype 5 - *The Wise Person/Thinker*

"It is a cursed evil to any man to become as absorbed in any subject as I am in mine."
– Charles Darwin.

"Joy in looking and comprehending is nature's most beautiful gift."
– Albert Einstein.

Type Fives want to understand how everything works and why. They want to use their knowledge to make the world a better place.

Core Value: Wisdom, knowledge, and learning. They like to know the rules, the expectations, and the guidelines of a situation. They want to be helpful and competent.

Ross believes he had a great childhood, "Mom was always there to keep me company and help me with my games and my schoolwork."

On further discussion, he admits that sometimes he would have loved some space to just be on his own. As an only child, he felt over-parented and micro-managed by his whole extended family, like he was the only thing they had to keep themselves entertained. Everything he did was observed, and he wasn't left to make his own mistakes. Before he even knew what he needed, his over-attentive family would be giving it to him or doing it for him - to help him.

"I think they thought they were helping me, but it made me feel like I wasn't able to do things by myself like I wasn't clever enough. I just wanted to prove that I could do stuff on my own and that I didn't need anyone's help. To prove I was clever enough to be given some independence."

Ross started using his intellect to create a mental and emotional distance between him and his family, just to get some breathing space. It became all about showing them he could do it by himself.

Core Fear: Being useless. Not knowing what to do. Looking foolish. Being annihilated or invaded and taken over by others. Losing themselves.

Core Weakness: Overly sensitive and protective of their space, they guard themselves by withdrawing from others and creating an intellectual barrier between them and the world. They can be secretive and isolated.

Maladaptive behavior: When Fives feel overwhelmed or inadequate, they retreat further into themselves. They can use contempt and intellect to protect themselves. They use logic - and will rationalize or trivialize to keep the upper hand.

Deep down, they don't have faith in themselves - that faith their parents didn't show in them by allowing them to be competent individuals.

Their parents didn't believe in them, and secretly neither did they. They need to work harder, know more, and be clever enough to overcome this perceived weakness. Knowledge helps them feel safer, but they also feel lonely and disconnected.

They tend to have a scarcity mentality - greedy for information, knowledge, and skills. They may also be stingy with sharing ideas, time, and energy. After all, it's their hard-won knowledge, which gives them an advantage - they think.

They hate it when people intrude on what they perceive as their tasks or area of expertise.

They just want to be left alone. They tend to be loners who view life from the sidelines. They battle to connect emotionally and live mainly in their heads rather than their hearts.

Core Strengths: Objective and observant - a Five can embody the Zen goal of non-attachment. They are perceptive and innovative.

Adaptive Behavior: Fives realize that it's safe to connect and that people value them for themselves and believe in them, regardless of how much they know. Real knowledge comes from wisdom, experience, and connection with others.

Calm and collected, Fives are very fair and good at analyzing situations clearly. They can work with systems and a large amount of information, distilling it down to its essential components. They are happy to be alone but have learned to allow others into their world too.

Key Developmental Areas:

1. Listening to others' points of view.
2. Understanding and recognizing emotions in themselves and others.
3. Assimilating emotions back into their world as a useful source of data and growth.
4. Allowing themselves to feel their feelings.
5. Learning to recognize when they are withdrawing and choose to connect instead.
6. "I am powerful and competent," replaces "I need to know more to be competent enough."

Possible Careers: They are best in an environment that allows them space to think, learn, and use their specific talents. Common jobs include engineering, math, writers, computer programmers, scientists, technicians, and scholars, or university professors.

Physical Signs of Type Five:

1. They will spend forever planning rather than doing.
2. Prefer their own company.
3. Have loads of books.
4. You can't get their attention when they're stuck in a book.
5. Really calm in a crisis.
6. Will pick out the one error in your otherwise perfect 12-page report.
7. They may be computer buffs and spend a lot of time in front of their screens.
8. Can appear cold and guarded.
9. Can't handle emotional displays.
10. If you ask them what they are feeling, they will tell you what they are thinking.

Famous Type Fives: Bill Gates, Jane Austen, Albert Einstein, Agatha Christie, Mark Zuckerberg.

What TV Characters Match this Type?

Rory Gilmore in *The Gilmore Girls*.

Severus Snape in *Harry Potter*.

Enneatype 6 - *The Loyal Person*

"I used to be more paranoid and stressed, constantly worrying about my Plan B. But the truth is, I don't have one."
– Uma Thurman.

"A lot of people give up just before they're about to make it. You know you never know when that next obstacle is going to be the last one."– Chuck Norris.

Type Six can be relied upon to always keep their word. If they make a commitment, they will follow through if it's at all possible.

Core Value: Loyalty, faithfulness, conscientiousness, and responsibility. Security, guidance, and support.

Amy found herself in juvenile detention at a young age. She had taken part in a protest rally. Things got out of hand, and she was caught breaking into and looting local shops with some other kids in the protest group.

She had grown up with a military father who had moved her from army base to army base, never settling anywhere for long. Although he was required to be authoritarian as part of his job as a ranking officer, he tried very hard to be a good and gentle parent. However, he found it difficult to not revert to ordering his family around and battled to distinguish between normal teenage personality development and unacceptable rebellion.

He blames himself for the fact his daughter, now in her twenties, is involved in a fringe group which is very anti-establishment. She now has a criminal record, and he worries that she will end up with a life sentence next time she is caught. She refuses to listen to reason.

Core Fear: Being seen as a coward or untrustworthy. Having no support, stability, or guidance.

They have been taught that the world is dangerous, and they either need to get authority on their side or oppose it. They gravitate towards being in a group to be safe.

Core Weakness: Anxiety about what could happen next.

Maladaptive behavior: Maladapted Sixes live in a constant state of apprehension about what could go wrong.

They need support and guidance. They need something to be loyal to. They need clarity. Predictable, safe environments attract them - even if it is just safety in numbers. They can be dogmatic, fanatic, and hard to shift if they believe they are right. They do not like their positions challenged or questioned. They can be quite fearful and reactive based on fear - and this underlies most of their choices.

Core Strengths: Strong belief in self, courage, and commitment. Hard-working and responsible.

Adaptive Behavior: Sixes are the best people to have at your back. They are great in a crisis, and always prepared.

They are trustworthy and responsible. They have an inner strength and take responsibility for their actions and beliefs. Their intuition for danger is highly developed.

Their strength comes from being in touch with themselves as well as reality. Extremely stable, they can be trusted to behave consistently and reliably. Their word is gold.

Once they realize that the world is not as dangerous as they believe and let go of their fears, they can apply both logic and feelings, and then can see other's perspectives. They no longer must cling so tightly to a security blanket.

Key Developmental Areas:

1. Living in the now versus worrying about an unknown future.
2. Managing anxiety by not overthinking.
3. Exploring fears and putting systems in place to help minimize worry and worst-case thinking.
4. Trusting intuition.
5. Taking back their power and trusting their own abilities and strength.
6. Believing in themselves.
7. Getting all the facts and asking questions before deciding on a polarizing issue.
8. "I am, therefore I am brave." replaces "I have to be loyal to be safe."

Possible Careers: Caregiver, lawyer or police force, administrator, banker, government official.

Physical Signs of Type Six:

1. Likes being in groups.
2. Someone's best friend.
3. In the front of the protest march.
4. At social gatherings and with those they love.
5. Really hates making decisions - can't tell you what they want for dinner.
6. Likes to be needed.
7. Have been in the same job for most of their life and won't hear a thing about their boss.
8. Married forever - or in one long-term relationship.

Famous Type Sixes: Tom Hanks, Ellen DeGeneres, Ben Affleck, JRR Tolkien.

What TV Characters Match this Type?

Robin Buckley in *Stranger Things*.
Ron Weasley *in Harry Potter*
Winnie the Pooh

Enneatype 7 - The Enthusiast

"Once we believe in ourselves, we can risk curiosity, wonder, spontaneous delight, or any experience that reveals the human spirit."– E. E. Cummings.

"On stage, it was always comfortable for me, because that's where I felt at home."– Elton John.

Type Sevens are all about optimistically enjoying life. They pursue delight on every level - looking for variety, excitement, and all the experiences life has to offer.

Core Value: Satisfaction and happiness.

Shelley was a happy-go-lucky little girl. She was petite, cute, and had the most adorable golden curls and big, blue eyes. She was clever, precocious, and funny.

Her parents loved trotting her out at all their parties and events as their little mascot. The "oohs" and "aahs" got her and her parents loads of approval and attention.

She quickly learned that entertaining people carried all kinds of rewards. She also learned that smiles and laughter got the best kind of attention - not tears or tantrums. So, she never showed that side of herself because it didn't work as well.

Her favorite saying is, "You catch more flies with honey than vinegar."

Core Fear: Pain and suffering. Deprivation. Fear of missing out (FOMO).

Core Weakness: Gluttony - an insatiable desire to fill the emptiness inside with something. But nothing has worked.

Maladaptive Behavior: Fulfillment is always just around the corner - the next experience, next lover, next gourmet meal, and so on.

When options become limited, Sevens get nervous. They need continual distractions and avoid acknowledging anything unpleasant.

Under stress, Sevens avoid dealing with reality. They will use anything to distract themselves and are resentful if life starts getting too hard, boring, or limited.

Core Strengths: Optimistic, creative, and full of fun, Sevens appreciate and enjoy life. Visionaries and great motivators. They are goal-oriented, engaged with life, and open to new ideas.

Adaptive Behavior: Sevens achieve harmony when they realize that reality is in the present moment, and only by fully being in this moment can you feel fulfilled. Accepting what is more satisfying than trying to forever achieve a fantasy.

Living a balanced and mindful life in the present achieves the happiness they used to chase.

Going for depth and awareness of the present experience to find satisfaction, instead of jumping from experience to experience.

They know their needs can be taken care of in the present moment, with what they have at hand.

Key Developmental Areas:

1. Completing projects.
2. Facing reality and confronting unpleasant situations and feelings.
3. Getting in touch with and accepting negative emotions.
4. Living in the now and appreciating what they have.

5. Realizing fulfillment isn't somewhere else.
6. Taking the time to listen to others fully.
7. Slowing down.

Possible Careers: Artist, travel guide, customer service of any sort, publicist, media consultant.

Physical Signs of Type Seven:

1. Enjoys being busy.
2. Has made plans for everyone in the house for the whole weekend, in advance.
3. Loves getting out and about, especially to parties, concerts and when around lots of new people.
4. Doesn't sit still.
5. Gets bored easily.
6. The life and soul of the party.
7. Impulsive.

Famous Type Sevens: Dick van Dyke, Elton John, Elizabeth Taylor, Jack Black, Oscar Wilde, Eddie Murphy.

What TV Characters Match this Type?

Frankie Bergstein in *Grace and Frankie.*

Tigger in *Winnie The Pooh.*

Fred and George Weasley in *Harry Potter.*

Enneatype 8 - The Protector/Challenger

"Speak softly and carry a big stick; you will go far."
– Theodore Roosevelt.

"I like a man who grins when he fights."
– Winston Churchill.

Type Eights desire power, strength, and influence. They are self-confident, assertive, and independent.

Core Value: To protect themselves and those they love, and to be in control of their lives.

Shireen had often been seen actually punching her co-workers. "I'm just sorting them out," she laughed, "It's just a joke!"

While some associates were juvenile enough to encourage this behavior, for everyone else, it was alarming and unacceptable.

When she couldn't get away with physical force, she bludgeoned people with passive aggression, stubbornness, or using policy and outright rudeness to show them she would not be pushed around. She had a reputation as being hot-headed, unhelpful, and obstructive.

She will tell anyone who asks, "I learned how to fight on the streets." Growing up in a poor neighborhood, with little adult supervision and some very tough kids on the block, she grew up with fists at the ready. This attitude has lasted well into adult life in some very unhelpful ways. She is kept in a back-office position, as out of the way of others as possible, and only her loyalty to the company keeps her in a job.

Core Fear: To be controlled or hurt by others. To be weak and powerless.

Core Weakness: They believe they must constantly defend themselves. They hate vulnerability and weakness.

Maladaptive Behavior: They rely on force and on being strong and tough to survive.

They can be quite confrontational.

They believe that they will be overlooked, ignored, excluded, or taken advantage of if they don't continually stand up for themselves. They see the world as dangerous and uncaring. If it doesn't give them what they need, they will take as much as they can grab and hold on to.

Denial of any weakness makes growth very difficult. To grow and learn, one needs to face yourself, but Eights don't like acknowledging what is wrong, so it can be quite hard to change for them.

Life is lived intensely - living, working, loving, fighting, and playing hard.

Kindness, sensitivity, empathy, and sentimentality are all seen as possible weaknesses.

They can be overbearing, intimidating, and sometimes bullying.

Core Strengths: Eights stand up for themselves and others. They are good at making hard and quick decisions and can clearly express themselves. They make good leaders and are both fair and logical.

Adaptive Behavior: Eights eventually realize that they don't have to fight so hard for justice. They know that karma and universal laws will ensure it without their personal guidance. Compassion and concern for others is balanced with attention to self.

They become more self-aware and open to accepting that their weaknesses can often also be hidden strengths, and that to know your weaknesses allows growth.

A move is made from external force towards inner power.

They learn they can trust, and they won't be betrayed.

Key Developmental Areas:

1. Put down the fists.
2. Let go - you can't control everything.
3. Work on trusting others.
4. Finding strength and value in gentleness and vulnerability.
5. Build others up.
6. Listening to and considering other ideas.
7. Allowing others to lead sometimes.
8. Go deep and discover all parts of the self. Be ok with acknowledging a weakness.
9. Work on expressing feelings.

Possible Careers: lawyer, politician, financial advisor, director or business owner.

Physical Signs of Type Eight:

1. They might give off quite a powerful, intimidating or bristly vibe - and wear this mask on purpose.
2. They hate taking blame.
3. They would make a good cage-fighter.
4. People are scared to take them on.
5. They don't follow orders so well - tend to prefer giving them.
6. Throw out other people's rule books.
7. Seldom say they are sorry.
8. Argumentative.

Famous Type Eights: Kathy Bates, Dr. Phil McGraw, Indira Gandhi, Donald Trump.

What TV Characters Match this Type?

Olivia Pope in *Scandal.*

King Arthur in *Merlin*

Harry Potter

Enneatype 9 - The Peacemaker

"I'm drawn to the path of least resistance." – Jeff Bridges.

"If you can, help others; if you cannot do that, at least do not harm them." – 14th Dalai Lama.

Type Nines want inner peace and harmony with themselves and the world.

Core Value: Wholeness and peace of mind.

Greg grew up in a very busy, noisy family. While his many brothers and sisters were fighting, yelling, jumping, playing, and just generally demanding, he retreated to a corner of his room with a book. "I think my parents were just relieved to have one kid they didn't have to worry about all the time," he says. As a result, everyone else got all the attention. Greg felt overlooked, left out, and neglected quite often. "There was even the time my mom forgot me at church for a whole afternoon because my brother wasn't with me, and because it was me on my own, she just forgot me."

You can hear the pain and resignation in his voice when he tells the story.

Core Fear: Loss and separation or disconnection.

Core Weakness: Nines dislike conflict or any form of tension. They worry that they will lose vital connections and may be excluded and rejected if they behave in a conflictual way.

Maladaptive Behavior: Nines can focus so intently in appearing to be calm and peaceful that they get stuck in permanent inaction. They minimize the importance of problems and how they feel about them so that they are not forced to face reality or must do something about it.

They can go on autopilot and be weak and ineffectual - resorting to no action instead of the wrong sort of possibly dangerous action. Indecisiveness, procrastination, pointless routines, and neglect of self and others can result.

As they fear conflict, they may resort to passive-aggressive behavior to get what they want or need.

"Nothing really matters," is their go-to saying. They resign and numb themselves to reality. After all, nothing can hurt you if you don't let it.

Nines can also become worried, obsessive, and fearful - needing outside authority to help direct and calm them.

Core Strengths: Diplomatic, supportive, harmonizing, intuitive, calm, reassuring, relaxed, and focused. Adaptive, open-minded, and nonjudgmental. They make great mediators.

Adaptive Behavior: Nines reach harmony when they realize the world is made up of opposites, and everything has a place - for order to exist, there must also be chaos.

They want to actualize and reach their highest potential - and do this best by connecting with self and others.

They learn that they do matter. They get in touch with their needs, wants, and desires and learn to act to achieve them.

Key Developmental Areas:

1. Discover what you want.
2. Develop a voice - ask for what you want or get clear about what you don't want.
3. Understand that conflict and pain is, at times, necessary for growth.

4. Learn to manage conflict for the best outcome rather than avoid it.
5. Work on self-acceptance.
6. Face and allow negative emotions.
7. Physical exercise helps ground a Nine.

Possible Careers: Counselors, vets, librarians, social workers, mediators, psychologists, psychiatrists, human resources, diplomats, writers, artists.

Physical Signs of Type Nine:

1. Can be easily distracted.
2. Avoids conflict.
3. Quiet and soft-spoken.
4. Will get more upset at being told they have disappointed you than they would at actual physical violence.
5. Never interrupts.
6. Good listeners.
7. Will be the one in the corner at a party listening to a friend's marital problems.

Famous Type Nines: Walt Disney, Barack Obama, Morgan Freeman, Abraham Lincoln, Jeff Bridges, Clint Eastwood.

What TV Characters Match this Type?

Pam Beesly in *The Office*

Albus Dumbledore in *Harry Potter*

Kanga in *Winnie the Pooh.*

The Funny Side of the Enneagram

The age-old joke – how many of a certain type does it take to screw in a lightbulb beautifully explains each Enneatype in the following excerpt:

Q: How many Ones does it take to screw in a light bulb?
A: Shouldn't we be using longer-lasting bulbs?

Q: Twos?
A: As many as you need!

Q: Threes?
A: Just one. But someone has to be watching.

Q: Fours?
A: One to screw in the bulb, and one to observe how little light it casts on the dark sea of despair in which we live.

Q: Fives?
A: That remains to be seen. No one can answer that question with any reasonable expectation of accuracy without further investigation. And it's possible that the question itself is flawed.

Q: Sixes?
A: Three. One to screw it in, one to unscrew it, and one to screw it back in.

Q: Sevens?
A: None! We brought fireworks!

Q: Eights?
A: None; Eights aren't afraid of the dark.

Q: Nines?
A: Oh, the old one is fine.

Part 2: Motivation, Fixing, and Resources

Each type can be more easily understood and summarized if we understand the type's primary motivation, fixation, and the strengths and resources they have available to them.

Motivation is the underlying driver of each type – it is the knee-jerk survival pattern a young child has decided is what is needed to be safe.

The fixation is where an Enneatype will focus their thoughts and energies.

Strengths are self-explanatory, and a type's Essence is what lies at their core when they are in a state of balance and growth.

Type 1

Motivation: Anger - experienced as a disturbance, which is based on dissatisfaction. It can range from mild irritation to hysterical anger and pure hatred.

Fixation: A condemnation in which dissatisfaction is expressed through internal criticism or in the form of comments in relation to other people. In addition, there is a tendency to denounce upcoming events and possible reactions to them.

Strength: Calmness is the ability to be happy and contented with inner harmony and peace, regardless of what is happening.

Essence: Perfection is an experience of the fact that everything in the Universe: things, events, people, and their behavior, is exactly what it should be - every moment is impeccable.

Type 2

Motivation: Pride is experienced as a feeling of satisfaction when you succeed, and you help other people.

Fixation: Gratitude - It is important for the "Two" to both express and receive gratitude. A smile, nod, or verbal admission that someone has said or done something good.

Strength: Modesty is the realization that it is not only my merit, and I'm only part of something bigger.

Essence: Freedom - I do not depend on the appreciation of others—the freedom to help and get help.

Type 3

Motivation: Deception is self-deception when you begin to play a role in order to gain inner value and significance. To do this, you "turn off" your emotions and concentrate on goals and outcomes.

Fixation: Vanity - experienced as the importance of status, image, and fashion. It is important to look good and make a good impression both in appearance and in competence.

Strength: Honesty is the ability to be completely honest, to do actions based on true emotions.

Essence: Hope - experienced as faith in the future. Understanding that I do not need to do anything, everything will be fine anyway.

Type 4

Motivation: Envy - experienced as an inner void, loss - something is missing for me.

Fixation: Longing - rich inner fantasies and a world of dreams, in comparison with which reality seems boring, something is missing in it. Type 4 flies into idealized dreams or memories of the past.

Strength: Balance is a state of emotional stability. I am more than my feelings. Equality is also - each person is equal and unique.

Essence: Unity - the experience of connecting everything with everything in the Universe; no one is ever alone.

Type 5

Motivation: Greed - it is felt as a lack or limited availability of resources of energy, knowledge, space, love, etc.

Fixation: Removal / isolation - a reaction to limited resources, which makes type 5 cherish what they have, and to avoid situations when others expect something from them - because this means that they will have to lose some of their accumulated resources.

Strength: Generosity is experienced as a strong emotional love for people and the world, thanks to which type 5 sacrifices time and resources to create something good in the world.

Essence: Omniscience is the feeling that any resource is available just when there is a need for it, that everything in the Universe is part of a common stream.

Type 6

Motivation: Fear - is not felt directly but manifests itself as a state of constant anxiety and bad premonition. Subconscious motivation: a sense of danger.

Fixation: Doubt - controls the mind, type 6 constantly analyzes, finds contradictions in his and other people's opinions, intentions, and incompetence.

Strength: Courage is a tremendous inner strength to act, despite all the inner insecurity - the courage to believe that everything will be fine.

Essence: Faith is the realization that there is a Higher Power in the Universe that protects all living beings and that this Power exists in all living things.

Type 7

Motivation: Gluttony is the feeling that the world has an infinite number of possibilities and the need to use them all.

Fixation: Planning is a way to avoid anxiety by distracting your consciousness. Constant mental activity, many things simultaneously occupy the 7th type of consciousness.

Strength: Common sense is the ability to remain in the present without expectations, disturbing emotions, and thoughts.

Essence: Sensuality - the experience of unity and communication with everything through feelings and sensations. Staying in the present, full of joy.

Type 8

Motivation: Lust is a strong need to capture and possess. What type 8 seeks to capture can vary power - control - people - authority - food, etc.

Fixation: Justice is the feeling that responsibility for peace rests on their shoulders. This responsibility has no limits, and it is necessary to constantly fight for what you want to receive.

Strength: Innocence is the feeling that everything is in balance and that no one is to blame.

Essence: Truth is the realization that everything that happens is a combination of chances caused by the natural course of things—a condition in which exemption and relinquishment of control give real effect.

Type 9

Motivation: Laziness is an internal need to stay inactive, relax, wait, and see what happens.

Fixation: Inaction - the desire to be calm and detached in order to avoid conflict. An attempt to create and maintain a sense of peace in all possible ways, always and everywhere.

Strength: Energy - manifests itself in spontaneous instinctive actions, not suppressed by thoughts or emotions, you are driven by instinct.

Essence: Love - the feeling that everything in the Universe is made of love and driven by love; - this power is everything and the cause of everything.

Enneagram of Vices

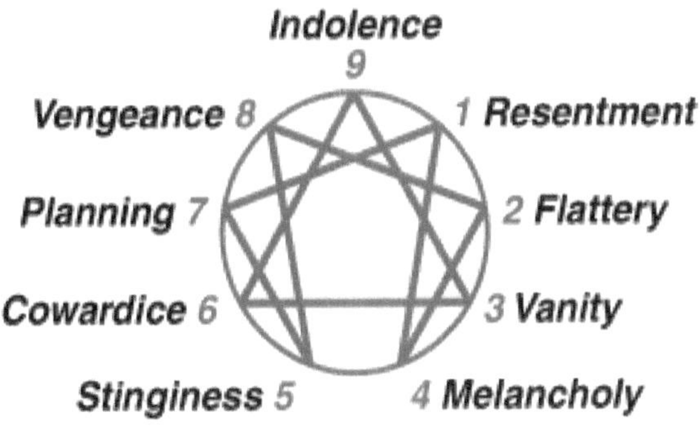

Enneagram of Virtues

Part 3: What is a Wing in an Enneagram?

It is possible that your Enneatype is modified - or leans towards - either of the types to either side of yours. So, a 9 could have a wing of an 8 or a 1, for example.

It is often written 9W1 or 9W8.

Because types do not exist in a hard and fast category, but more in a spectrum of behavior and context, you might find you are closer to one wing or another on the Enneatype spectrum.

Your Enneatype tests generally help you to define what your wing may be. And you will find that although your core type is the most dominant, you are also influenced to a lesser degree by your wing Enneatype.

It is useful to know this when considering your vices and virtues and how you might find your true essential state of harmony.

Part 4: Transitions Under Stress and Security

The next important thing to understand about the Enneagram is that the arrows connecting each type are a vital tool to help you understand how an Enneatype might react under stress.

When a person is exposed to a challenging situation, more than the usual challenges they are used to, they might transition towards a corresponding type's vice.

Conversely, when an Enneatype is very relaxed, secure, happy, and open to growth, they might transition towards another type as well.

Suddenly the strange and occult lines make more sense—these lines show which types transition where and how.

The diagram below shows how this works.

So, a Nine, under high stress, might transition towards a type Six and start being fixated with rules and loyalties. But when relaxed and feeling secure, they might be more like a type Three, where they are happy to be in the limelight and more creative and expressive.

So, altogether an Enneatype can be affected both by its wings and by its stress or security points - making a total of four possible types influencing a person's behavior.

THE ENNEAGRAM

How does each type react when they are put into a stress or security situation?

Type 1

Stress

When you come under pressure and become unsure, you can recognize the patterns of behavior of the 4th type. You easily lose your self-esteem and feel that problems overshadow everything. You get access to your emotions and remember all those cases when something did not work out. At the same time, you become aware of the emotions of other people, as well as how they perceive your behavior.

Security

When you feel like in seventh heaven, full of resources, and are safe, then you use patterns of behavior of the 7th type. You have a lot of ideas, you enjoy planning upcoming events, and you dream about what you might want to do in the future. You are freed from the need to bring everything to perfection, and it becomes easier for you to accept everything as it is, without correcting anything.

Type 2

Stress

When you are pressured, and you are not confident enough in yourself, you begin to show the character traits of the 8th type and fall into aggression faster. Suddenly, you are sure that you need what you want and begin to control the situation in a style that surprises your loved ones. Justice becomes important to you, and you may feel that others do not respect you.

Security

When you feel safe, and in a resource state, you begin to show patterns of behavior of the 4th type. You become more creative and more easily aware of what is important to you. You begin to appreciate the intensity (severity of feelings) and intimacy; it becomes important for you to take an individual approach to business, do everything in your own special way.

Type 3

Stress

If you are experiencing emotional pressure or exhaustion, you are exhibiting behaviors of the 9th type. Suddenly, it becomes difficult for you to prioritize; all tasks become equally important. It is difficult for you to finish the job, and it seems to you that you are running in a circle, and nothing is working out.

Security

When you are safe, and in a resource state, you exhibit behaviors of the 6th type. You realistically evaluate your tasks, given the time and resources available to you. It becomes easy for you to analyze the consequences and take a sound skeptical approach to business.

Type 4

Stress

If you are under pressure and feel insecure, then you begin to show stereotypes of type 2 behavior. You lose touch with your emotions and cease to be confident in what you want. Unexpectedly for you, it becomes easier for you to pay attention to the needs of other people, and you notice that you are adapting to the desires of other people.

Security

Being safe and in a resource state, you begin to show patterns of behavior of the 1st type. You can focus on the task and forget your concern with yourself and other people's opinions about yourself. Now you direct all your attention to the task. You pay more attention to details and love to perfect everything.

Type 5

Stress

When you are under pressure and feel that your boundaries are being violated, you gain access to stereotypes of the behavior of the 7th type. You lose your inner balance, and unrealistic ideas begin to overwhelm you, which leads you into a state of uncertainty. You begin to superficially treat problems, become an extrovert. This gives you the feeling that you do not respect yourself and others.

Security

When you feel confident, safe, you get access to stereotypes of the behavior of the 8th type. You begin to command more, easily take control into your own hands. Now it's easy for you to make sure that your needs are met, and you can be very charming. Your usual strategy to think about something is replaced by action.

Type 6

Stress

When you are under pressure or threatened, you begin to use stereotypes of type 3 behavior. You become more active, but at the same time experiencing frustration, because you are not able to thoroughly think about what is happening before making a decision.

Security

When you feel safe and trust, you use the 9th type of behavior model. You become slower and begin to accept what is, begin to see mostly good things in people. Your skepticism recedes, in its place, comes the feeling: "better just enjoy each other's company."

Type 7

Stress

When you are under pressure and feel that choices are limited, you begin to show patterns of behavior of the 1st type. You can no longer perceive the whole situation and begin to pay attention to the details of a specific task. It's easier to make you angry, and you begin to condemn yourself and others more.

Security

When you are full of resources and experiencing an emotional upsurge, you use the 5th type of behavior models, become more introverted and thoughtful. It becomes more important to spend time collecting knowledge, and you like to spend time alone with a good book.

Type 8

Stress

When you are under pressure or feel that you have "bitten off more than you can chew," you begin to show patterns of behavior of the 5th type - you step back, thinking about new ways to act. You move away from others and do not pull them into your personal problems and sorrows.

Security

When you are safe and can "lay down your arms," you begin to show patterns of behavior of the 2nd type and pay more attention to the needs of other people. Then you are very courteous, take good care of loved ones and those in need.

Type 9

Stress

When you are under pressure, you start using behaviors of the 6th type and begin to be more skeptical about the motives of others. It becomes difficult for you to trust your own judgments, and you analyze the situation again and again.

Security

When you feel safe and feel harmony, you are exhibiting type 3 behavior patterns. You concentrate on the task before you, on what needs to be done, and on important goals. You become very productive.

Part 5: What You Need to Remember About Enneatypes

I think I am a bit of all the types.

You might be thinking that you picked up a bit of every type in yourself, so how can it be right? The Enneagram is very flexible - and does not force you into a box. Everyone is going to have their own combination - with different wing dominance and so on. And it is quite common to see a bit of each type in ourselves.

On one level, this makes other paths more relatable and recognizable - so it's good if you can empathize with other types.

However, you will have only one main type - which you will return to again and again. This main type remains unchanged throughout our lives. Even when you change and develop, it will remain your main type.

Does gender affect Enneatype?

Descriptions of personality types are universal and apply equally to men and women. Of course, men and women can display the same features, reactions, and their attitude to events in different ways; however, the main signs and characteristics of the type remain unchanged.

Some of the descriptions of my type definitely don't apply to me?

Not all descriptions of your basic type will suit you constantly. This is due to our constant transition from a healthy level to an unhealthy one, and back, which forms our personality type. We will also see that our personal growth or increasing stress plays a crucial role in the way we manifest our type.

Why do the Enneatype names differ depending on the source?

Even though we assigned a name to each type, in practice, we prefer to number Enneatypes. These numbers are neutral in their significance, and the numbers themselves are not on a scale and do not show a rating. The type of person with a large number is no better than the type with a smaller number.

Is there a preferred Enneatype?

None of the personality types is any better than the other - each type has its own advantages and disadvantages, strengths and weaknesses. However, representatives of certain types may be more valued in a society or culture.

With a deeper study of personality types, you will see that just as everyone has unique capabilities, everyone has different limitations.

No matter what main type you belong to, you will have more or less of the features of all nine types.

To explore and discover the work of each of them within us is to understand the whole spectrum of human nature. Such awareness will give you a deeper understanding of and compassion for others, as you will find many habits and their characteristic reactions in yourself.

It is much more difficult to condemn the aggression of an Eight, for example, or the desire of the Twos to be needed when we see similar things in ourselves. If you examine the presence of all Nine types in yourself, you will see how much they are interdependent and interchangeable, exactly as the symbol of the Enneagram represents.

It is the process of developing self-awareness and understanding the virtue and vice of each type that will be most useful.

For example, when we see a pattern of anger in ourselves - to know it's the motivation of a One, might give us insight into that anger and what we can do to counter and shift it.

Chapter 3: The Three Types of Intelligence

The Nine types fall into three triads - the feeling (emotional), the thinking (mental), and the instinctive (body).

The Enneatypes within each triad is governed mainly by that type of intelligence - either emotional, instinctual, or by reason.

Although we all have access to all three types of intelligence - our Enneatype will decide the type of intelligence we mainly revert to using. Basically, one type will be more used and, therefore, more developed for each person.

Your leading center also will give you insight into which path you could take to be more effective.

Thinking Triad: Types Five, Six, and Seven are head-centered types.

Rational thought, ideas, and a need for clarity underline their choices and actions. This is how they feel safe in the world. Fear drives all they do.

Fives over express thought. Sixes are detached or out of touch with their own inner guidance, and Sevens under express their thoughts - rushing in without thinking enough.

What works for them: When healthy. They are incredibly insightful, have great ideas, and are very perceptive.

What they need to do less of: The downside is that this type can become over-analytical, and fearful of taking action through over-thinking and imagining the worst.

Instinctive Triad: Types Eight, Nine, and One are guided more by their gut or instinctive insight. The instincts of the body and survival rule them.

Eights over-express, Nines are out of touch, and Ones under-express their instinctive energies.

What works for them: when healthy, they relate well to the environment and to others. They can be deeply wise.

What they need to do less of: This triad resists what is and tries to control their world to make it safe. Their underlying feeling is one of rage, and they have aggression and repression issues. They can deny reality and try to replace it with what they want.

Feeling Triad: Types Two, Three, and Four are more emotional and centered in their hearts.

They rely on feelings to make sense of their world and to give them guidance. Self-image underlies their choices. They use it for protection. Shame drives them - emotionally trapping them in the past.

Twos over-express (positive) feelings, Threes are out of touch with their feelings, and Fours under-express their feelings.

What works for them: When healthy, their feelings provide excellent data about the world and others. They can truly empathize and connect via emotions.

What they need to do less of: They can also be overly sensitive or insensitive and use emotions to manipulate others.

You will find it easier to communicate with people from your own Triad, but relationships across Triads brings growth and complements your strengths with their diversity.

If you can learn to balance and harmonize strengths from all three triads - when your heart, head, and gut are aligned, you will feel more balanced and at peace. It will also add an extra dimension to your ability to function in the world.

Which is my Triad?

Do you:

1. Get angry easily at small or random things?
2. Get scared by what you might unleash once you start digging into your thoughts and feelings?
3. Like to be independent?
4. Often use the words "should" or "should not?"
5. Like to be in control of things?

You could be in the Instinctive or Feeling Triad.

Do you:

1. Often feel worried about how others view you?
2. Need approval and attention?
3. Often ask, "Who am I?"
4. Resent people for not reciprocating your efforts?
5. Think about the past, and what you could have done better?

You could be in the Feeling Triad.

If you:

1. Have to think before you decide how you feel.
2. Think about the future a lot.
3. Worry and overthink.
4. Wonder, "What's going to happen to me?"
5. Have plans, and contingency plans, for every worst-case scenario you can imagine.

You could be in the Thinking Triad.

Chapter 4: Harmonizing Three Instincts in the Enneagram

You might be surprised, but in fact, the Enneagram is not limited to nine types, but in fact, can be split into 27 variants.

This flexibility in type is created by our instincts.

Each Enneatype also manifests in three main forms or primal instincts. Our deep motivations are generally linked to and influenced by one of the three.

What is an Instinct?

Instinct is hardwired into us via the animal parts of our brains that developed many thousands of years ago. Instincts like fight-or-flight, caring for our young, mating, and so on, are primal and survival-based. If we want to see how instinct can affect a living being, animals are a good example, as they live, survive, and thrive based wholly on instinct and not higher thinking processes.

Simply put, this is an unconscious impulse aimed at satisfying important needs. We have many instincts, but the three most important in the Enneagram are the instinct of self-preservation, social, and sexual needs.

Our dominating instinct in the Enneagram is what determines where most of our vital energy will be directed.

How are Instincts Related to Each Other?

Instincts manifest themselves in our lives in a certain way.

The three instincts are ordered in different levels of importance for each person.

If you were to visualize how the instincts relate, think of a pie, the upper layer of which is the dominant or leading instinct, the middle layer is the auxiliary instinct, and the lower layer is the blind spot, or the mostly unused sleeping instinct.

So, the three instincts, self-preservation, social, and sexual needs, will fall in a specific order for you.

Part 1: The Trinity

Self-Preservation

This is one of the most primal instincts and is responsible for our physical survival.

In animals, this instinct consists of two main aspects:

1. The need for food - any living organism needs to receive energy for life.
2. The need for rest - having obtained food, it is necessary to digest it, restore strength, and gain energy in a safe place.

For the animal to survive, it is vital that both needs are met.

For humans, we can see this instinct in more evolved ways. To obtain the food we need, to educate ourselves, groom ourselves, and create a means of stable income to buy the food. We need security - to make sure we can access the food when we need to.

Our social structures and our ability to create, invent, develop, and use tools and technology, create a complex net of must-have elements for us to survive.

Issues like economic and political stability, financial skills and choices, social skills, health, and more, all influence our self-preservation and are influenced by it.

Social Instinct

From the dawn of evolution, life began to unite in clumps of cells, and then into groups of organisms, because this increased their chances of survival.

In ancient human tribes, one of the worst punishments was the expulsion, as that meant near-certain death out in the dark and cold, denied the protection and resources of your people.

In modern life, social instinct manifests itself in the desire to be part of a group, to do something important for other people - and in return to receive the acceptance, recognition, and respect of the group.

Sexual instinct

In the Enneagram, we often call it the 1:1 instinct, to emphasize that it has only an indirect relation to sexuality and sex appeal.

Initially, this instinct is responsible for the attraction of one individual to another, but in modern life, it manifests itself primarily in the search for understanding and deep emotional closeness in personal relationships and friendship, as well as in the desire for intense feelings.

Part 2: Leading, Auxiliary, and Sleeping Instincts

Imagine that you came to a party in an unfamiliar company.

Depending on your leading instinct, your attention will be directed to different things.

If your leading instinct is the self-preservation instinct, then, first of all, you will pay attention to how physically comfortable you are here - whether you managed to find a comfy spot to sit, how tasty (or wholesome) the food is, what drinks are served, whether you're sitting in a draft, and so on.

If your leading instinct is social, then you will pay attention to people - and especially to relations between people in a group. You will quickly understand which of those present is in the spotlight, who is the most respected or who has more status, and it will be important for you to be closer to these people.

And if you feel comfortable enough, you may even begin to compete for the attention of the group.

You will meet as many new people as possible because you believe that social connections are interesting and very useful.

If your leading instinct is sexual, then it will be important for you to take a good look at the people around you and find among the guests one person who seems especially interesting and attractive to you (maybe even mysterious). You will spend almost the whole evening in an interesting and in-depth communication with this one person, and you will feel that a special understanding and emotional connection has been established between you.

Leading Instinct

Your leading instinct is the top layer of your instinctive pie. This is the area of your life that you devote most of your time and energy to. We are very different in values and interests, depending on our leading instinct.

Auxiliary Instinct

If the top layer of the pie is the dominant or leading instinct, the next is our secondary auxiliary instinct.

It is less important to us than our leading instinct, but still features in our life to some degree. We will not react as deeply or intensively when the needs associated with our secondary/auxiliary instinct are denied or frustrated.

The peculiarity of the auxiliary instinct is that when we experience a crisis in our leading instinct, we can temporarily switch to the secondary one and use it to compensate for frustration.

Imagine a person with a leading sexual instinct and an auxiliary instinct of self-preservation. Experiencing pain from a bad breakup, such a person can compensate for it with the physical pleasures of food. If in the same situation, the auxiliary instinct is social, then the person will most likely direct energy to work and social activity.

Sleeping Instinct

The last layer of the pie is our sleeping instinct.
The needs associated with it will not seem so important.

If they are satisfied, it will be without much effort on our part. And if they are frustrated, this will not really bother us.

We can take it or leave it.

For example, if you have self-preservation in the bottom layer of the pie, then you won't stress too much if you have to change jobs and will decide your next job based on social or sexual instinct rather than how much money or how stable it is.

Building relationships with others whose instincts match ours - whether a life partner, at work or among friends, will always feel easier and more natural because our values and hierarchy of needs match.

Leading Self-preservation Instinct

If your leading instinct is self-preservation, your focus is primarily aimed at satisfying basic material and physical needs.

You want good, comfortable housing, financial stability, good physical health, and a stable environment.

The greatest fear for people with a dominant instinct of self-preservation is the fear of losing stability, security, and comfort in life.

Great life stress for them would be the threat of losing their usual source of income, any changes that entail uncertainty, poor mental or physical health, or threats in their environment (social, political, environmental, and so on).

Leading social instinct

For people with a leading social instinct, the role and position they occupy in the group are vital. They are focused on whether their group accepts them and what value they have within the group. Gaining status and recognition in social groups and communities are what drives them.

A group can be a family, a social circle, a workplace, a team, a professional community, or even a country.

The biggest fear for people with this instinct is to be cast out or rejected by an important group for them. They experience stress when they feel that they are being excluded from the group, or if they might be losing their position in the group.

Leading sexual instinct

People with a dominant sexual instinct are looking for a partner who shares their most important values, who could literally become their 'second half.'

The same principle applies to their friendships.

It is also important for people with a sexual instinct to find 'their passion in life' - that work, or occupation, that they can connect too deeply.

They want deep, meaningful connections, meaning, and intensity in life.

The greatest fear for people with this instinct is to live their life disconnected and alone, without meaning or deep connection to others, their work, or their life purpose.

They fear never finding their second half. Or once they have found this person, they fear losing them.

They fear a meaningless life 'without a spark.' The inability to find something that really captivates them, or the inability to pursue it.

Part 3: Harmonization of Instincts

To achieve happiness and inner peace - we need to have all three instincts in balance.

Instincts describe the three most important areas of our lives, and ideally, all three should be satisfied. But often, an imbalance arises, depending on our childhood lessons.

As a result, we begin to suppress and ignore some areas of life, and some acquire super-value for us.

This imbalance is often unpleasantly manifested in our lives, for example, we direct all our energy into our work and making money (self-preservation), but we don't have any time or energy left for connection (sexual instinct).

Fortunately, with awareness, you can fix this.

Practical Exercise: Harmonizing and the Wheel of Balance Technique

One way to identify your dominant, secondary, and sleeping instincts is to use the "Wheel of Balance" technique.

1. Draw a circle and divide it into 3 sections or pie slices, writing in the three instincts (Self-preservation, sexual and social) in random order.

2. In each pie slice, write down what you hold important, that relates to that instinct. Aim for seven values per pie slice.

   To help you, try answering these questions for each instinct:

   - What is important to me in this area?
   - What brings me pleasure in this area?
   - What would I not want to lose in this area?

3. Pay special attention to deep, core values - what makes your life truly happy and fulfilled. Those things you simply cannot live without.

4. Decide which of the instincts is leading, which is auxiliary, and which is sleeping. To do this, for each area, answer the questions:
   - How much time of my life do I devote to this area?
   - How much energy do I spend on meeting needs in this area?
   - How much attention do I pay to issues related to this area?

5. Put a percentage number next to each of the areas based on the time and energy you devote to it (the sum of percentages for all three areas should be 100). Your dominant instinct would have the highest score, the sleeping instinct the lowest one.

6. Assess your satisfaction in each of the areas. To do this, in relation to each area, ask yourself the following questions:
   - How satisfied are my important values and needs in this area?
   - How happy do I feel in this area?
   - Which of my important needs in this area are not satisfied?

7. Put a percentage number next to each of the areas based on your satisfaction with it (the sum of percentages for all three areas should be 100). This is key to showing you which areas you might want to focus more attention on, to bring your life into balance.
8. Identify limiting beliefs in each of the instincts.

   - Highlight the values which seem incompatible - for example, "a successful career" and "family time."

- Make a note of the feelings you have about your values - do some seem 'good' and others 'bad?' Or "I do not deserve it," or "I will never have it."

Remember that our limiting beliefs are often irrational because most of them were formed in early childhood, based on our experiences, which are different for each person.

9. To discover more limiting beliefs, answer the following questions regarding each value you have listed:

   - What do I believe about this at the deepest level?
   - What beliefs may be causing my current situation in this area?
   - What did my parents believe about this area, and how did it affect me?
   - What decisions have I already made regarding this area (important decisions, most of which are made at an early age)?

Write it all down without second-guessing yourself, even if the answers seem simple or childish. Don't judge them; they are vital insights into your worldview and also into faulty thinking and limiting root beliefs that can now be changed.

Once you have done all this self-analysis - look at it as objectively as you can. Often at this point, when we see what we are thinking in black-and-white, we have an instant "aha" moment.

It is time to start the harmonizing process.

Practical Exercise: Harmonizing for Positive Change

Use the following exercise to help you analyze your beliefs and start the healing.

1. List all the root beliefs you have found for each value in your instinct pie.

2. Next to each belief write, "I believe this is so because . . ." and then write the answer.

3. Keep asking that of your answers until you believe you have got to the key or root of the issue. For example, I want a stable income, but I don't think that is possible because I have never had one before. I have never had one before because I keep changing jobs. I keep changing jobs because I get bored. I get bored because I think there is something better out there. I think there is something better out there because I haven't really explored the opportunities in my current job. I haven't really explored the opportunities because I am afraid that I will be shown up as stupid or fail at the new tasks. In a new job, people would be more understanding. In this example, the person has uncovered that their root belief is that they cannot do it, that they aren't good or clever enough.

4. Once you have uncovered as many of the root beliefs as you can - ask yourself what you could do to prove to yourself that this root belief just isn't so. In this example, the person could list all the achievements and successes they have had to date. Or they could choose some new, perhaps small, and achievable challenges, which they feel

more comfortable succeeding at, and once those are complete, go for bigger and bigger ones. This would all provide solid counter evidence to the root belief and help with letting it go and growing self-confidence.

5. For each root belief, think about what new behavior you can choose to support a different and more helpful, supportive belief.

6. Consider how you can bring greater balance to your three instincts and what new choices and habits you can create to do so.

Chapter 5: Pathways to Awareness and Development

Each Enneatype has a clear pathway they must take to grow, shift, and find happiness.

Depending on where a person is at with their growth, they may behave very differently to people in the same Enneatype but on a different level of growth. It really depends on each person's level of awareness, mental and emotional health. This determines what level they sit at, and what type of behavior you might expect from them. It also helps show the degree of their mental and emotional health. They are indicators of the degree of our freedom and awareness.

In 1977 Don Riso and Ross Hudson - Enneagram researchers - discovered that each type of Enneagram is not only characterized by the three main ranges of development: healthy, medium, unhealthy but that there are even more subtle differences. He came up with nine levels of development.

Ken Wilber, the creator of the Integral Approach, praised this discovery, pointing out that "by combining the horizontal types of Enneagram with the system of vertical levels of development, Riso and Hudson had created one of the first truly integral models of the human soul."

	Level 1	The Level of Liberation
Healthy	Level 2	The Level of Psychological Capacity
	Level 3	The Level of Social Value
	Level 4	The Level of Imbalance/ Social Role
Average	Level 5	The Level of Interpersonal Control
	Level 6	The Level of Overcompensation
	Level 7	The Level of Violation
Unhealthy	Level 8	The Level of Obsession and Compulsion
	Level 9	The Level of Pathological Destructiveness

If we are in a healthy range of levels, then we are less affected by ego and external circumstances. We can be present in the present, here and now, make the right choices and act effortlessly and wisely, and with strength and compassion, among other things.

In the intermediate range, we show those qualities and character traits that are considered "normal" or more typical behavior of the Enneatypes. This is the range in which the average person, who hasn't done much self-awareness work, will function. They identify with their type strongly, and their emotional balance depends heavily on external circumstances.

The unhealthy range represents the most destructive manifestations of Enneatype behavior. People at these levels tend to be counter-productive, destructive and destructive, lose touch with reality and fall into a maze of reactions and illusions. They are unable to control anything and usually cannot change their behavior without the help of specialists.

What Type of Behavior Occurs at Each Level?

We have broken down the typical behavior at each level for each type, starting at level seven and showing how awareness grows and change occurs up until level one.

Type 1

The development path for type 1 is to recognize your emotions and impulses and realize that negative emotions quickly disappear when you accept them. Thus, type 1 can be freed from the desire to condemn everyone, and instead feel peace and clarity, leading to a state of true existence in which everything is perceived as perfect and subordinate to a higher "order."

Type 2

The development path for type 2 is to learn to trust yourself and learn to ask and receive help from others. In this way, they gain double access to their virtue - modesty. Thanks to this, the deuce can survive such a manifestation of true existence in which there is the freedom to give and receive while remaining at the same time.

Type 3

The development path for type 3 is to be completely honest with yourself and others. It is necessary to develop access to your emotions and work on the conviction "I am loved regardless of whether I did something or not, whether I am successful or not." Thanks to this, the 3rd type gains access to a special manifestation of genuine existence, in which it comes to the realization that everything is developing in the right direction, and that one person cannot do everything.

Type 4

The path of development for the 4th personality type is based on their special ability to perceive that everything around is equal. It is necessary to pay attention to what is now and to realize that it is as valuable and attractive as what is currently missing. This is how Type 4 people feel that they don't have to suffer and get access to this manifestation of true existence in which they feel connected to everything.

Type 5

The development path for the 5th type is to generously share resources and yourself - then the 5th type opens an endless source of knowledge and energy. Then it becomes possible to establish a connection with a special manifestation of the true Being, which we call omniscience. Omniscience is the ability to feel connected with a higher mind and see life as a whole.

Type 6

The development path for type 6 is to get rid of doubt and develop trust. This will provide an opportunity to access such a manifestation of the Essence, in which there is a strong belief that "everything is going well."

Type 7

The development path for the 7th type is to stay "here and now," no matter what this moment is. Due to this, the 7th type develops a special ability – to soberly perceive reality.

Type 8

The development path for type 8 is to build a connection with the vulnerable inner side, where the "soft" emotions are. The 8th type should develop in itself the ability to simply be in the present, not trying to influence the situation, take control, or responsibility.

Type 9

The developmental path for type 9 is to develop the ability to act right now, and it is also necessary to develop the ability to communicate clearly and clearly with others, even if this can lead to conflict.

While our main Enneatype does not change throughout life, we can change our level of development. We can develop by integrating internal conflicts, changing our way of thinking, and working out our fears.

Changing our patterns and moving to a higher level is an essential and important step on the path of personal development and is felt like a cardinal change in character, behavior, and attitudes. This is a lasting change that cannot go unnoticed.

Chapter 6: Managing Conflict with Enneagram

Type Ones

Do:

- Take them seriously
- Understand what they believe to be right
- Respect their time
- Be clear - know what you are going to say
- Be gentle and constructive giving feedback = be specific
- Admit your own mistakes
- Express how you feel
- Encourage them to share their thoughts and feelings
- Allow them to take some time to reflect

Don't:

- Make fun of them
- Be harsh or blunt
- Rush them
- Waffle on and be unclear or vague

Type Twos

Do:

- Be accepting of them as people
- Be specific about the behavior you don't like - don't make it personal
- Be directly or overly critical - build them up rather than breaking them down
- Attentive and encouraging
- Share your perspective and let them share theirs fully - listen
- Show appreciation for them
- Take a problem-solving approach
- Recognize their strengths and contributions
- Share concerns sensitively
- Be polite and courteous and follow the correct forms of social interaction

Don't:

- Be overly critical
- Be insensitive to them and their feelings
- Neglect or reject them
- Overwhelm them

Type Threes

Do:

- Show appreciation for their strengths and good points while also showing how they might improve
- Be straightforward and clear
- Be concise
- Use constructive criticism
- Help them understand what you need or feel
- Give clear actions steps and assign responsibility for each one
- Encourage them to consider their feelings and to respect yours

Don't:

- Be vague or indirect
- Get personal or attack their character
- Use love and acceptance as a bargaining chip
- Denigrate or dismiss their achievements

Type Fours

Do:

- Ask their opinion and potential solutions
- Encourage them to share and not withdraw
- Focus on what is going right and how to improve what is not
- Stay calm if they get emotional - allow them space and time to decompress before continuing
- Ask them how you can help them
- Share your feelings
- Be optimistic and encouraging
- Be authentic and expressive
- Frame negative feedback as a chance to grow
- Empathize

Don't:

- Make them feel insignificant
- Blindly agree
- Disrespect their individuality
- Insist on resolving conflict when they are clearly emotional
- Let them withdraw for too long
- Be overly logical.

Type Fives

Do:
- Focus on one problem at a time
- Provide all the details
- Explain the effects of the problem on your emotions and what happens thereafter as a result
- Find areas of similarity and connection
- Give them lots of space and time to think
- Be clear and logical
- Ask them for their insights
- Be honest about growth areas
- Ask them to consider both sides
- Get them working with you to find a win-win or compromise

Don't:
- Let them withdraw for too long
- Let them talk over you - agree to a fair method of discussion
- Be overly emotional
- Get side-tracked
- Make excessive or unreasonable demands
- Force resolution immediately - agree on a time and place that suits all parties.

Type Sixes

Do:

- Appreciate their efforts
- Be supportive and encouraging
- Build trust
- Ask them how they see the problem
- Ask them how they think it might affect others - and help them understand that
- Be clear about the next steps and outcomes
- Help them plan out the next steps
- Remind them of what they have achieved
- Focus on what has gone well
- Listen and offer support
- Be calm and logical
- Help them feel safe to express themselves
- Stick to the schedule or agenda
- Let them help where they can
- Show them where they are needed
- Explain the purpose of the discussion upfront
- Remind them of other, similar issues which had a favorable outcome

Don't:

- Threaten them with vague dangers
- Magnify or dramatize problems
- Focus on failures
- Small talk
- Discourage and attack
- Be overly hard or harsh
- Be clear about the next steps and outcomes

Type Sevens

Do:

- Include them
- Let them brainstorm with you
- Encourage them to slow down and take their time before answering
- Be upbeat and optimistic
- Listen to them
- Show appreciation for their ideas
- Be clear about what is needed
- Allow casual conversation and dialogue

Don't:

- Be too long-winded or boring
- Be overly negative
- Let them rush too much
- Take up all the airspace
- Get too serious
- Take away all their freedom of choice
- Restrict them with too many rules and routines

Type Eights

Do:

- Create boundaries
- Try reason with emotion
- Discuss acceptable and unacceptable methods of discussion
- Negotiate a method for everyone to get a chance to speak
- Encourage them to use active and empathetic listening skills
- Be respectful to avoid defensiveness
- Call them out on inappropriate actions
- Be upfront and direct
- Be open to their ideas and consider their side
- Show respect and due consideration for their ideas
- Be logical and practical
- Highlight the worth of admitting weakness and identifying growth points

Don't:

- Be intimidated by them
- Be dismissive of them
- Let them take charge when it's not their turn or place
- Try bossing them around
- Blame - be inclusive of shared responsibilities for problems
- Get all your facts first
- Waffle or get side-tracked

Type Nines

Do:

- Be accepting of them
- Be agreeable, reassuring and supportive
- Ask them for their input
- Provide a safe space for them to share
- Reinforce that conflict is necessary for growth sometimes
- Communicate your purpose clearly
- Allow small-talk and connection
- Ask them what they need
- Be calm and patient
- Be gentle

Don't:

- Be too loud, aggressive or domineering
- Allow them to avoid issues for too long
- Pressure them
- Be overly negative or critical
- Force or rush hard decisions
- Shut them down

Chapter 7: Improving Relationships with Enneagram

Enneagram is so useful at helping us navigate the tricky waters of relationships.

How we show love, what each type looks for, and values in their relationships and what they find attractive is key to understanding why and how you are relating to your nearest and dearest.

Type Ones

What Does Love and Happiness Mean for This Type?

These people need to feel that everything is right, good, and orderly.

They want a relationship that flows in a predictable and organized fashion - with no nasty surprises.

They want love, approval, and acceptance.

What Attracts a Type One?

They love logic, honesty, and a practical, predictable, sensible character. Someone who is open-minded and relaxed and who also shares their views and values is ideal.

Open communication, support, and being supportive and involved in their and your own personal growth work well for them.

Do:

- Keep your agreements; be precise and punctual.

- Show them that you still love them, even when they are angry.
- Use praise and inspiration, rather than constant criticism.
- In a conflict situation, show that you are looking for a way to solve the problem constructively.
- Give tokens of appreciation - whether gifts, time, or attention.
- Remind them that you don't need perfection, that everything is already wonderful.
- Support regular rest and relaxation.

Type Twos

What Does Love and Happiness Mean for This Type?

Twos need to be fully loved and accepted and reminded of that. They need someone who is attentive to their needs, nurturing, and shows frequent appreciation.

What Attracts Type Two:

Kindness, empathy, open communication, and someone who will recognize and attend to their needs. They love cuddles and intimacy.

Do:

- Thank them for their help and understanding. And then thank you again.
- Show them how much you need them.
- Show an interest in their life and their problems and not allow them to shift the focus of attention to your affairs all the time.
- Talk often and deeply about feelings and wants.
- Encourage them to learn to accept help.

Support their creative impulses.

Type Threes

What Does Love and Happiness Mean for This Type?

They love open, driven relationships where there is a common goal that everyone is working toward.

What Attracts Type Three?

A partner who is as driven as them, and who understands and appreciates what they have done and are still trying to accomplish.

Do:

- Recognize their achievements and successes.
- Show understanding and gratitude for their efforts.
- Give them space when they are busy or join in and actively help if they will let you.
- Give them honest and objective feedback.
- Respect their feelings.
- Avoid rehashing their past mistakes.
- Work together on common goals. Joint productive activity unites them with partners.
- Encourage them to slow down and relax more often, because they are often in a hurry.
- Inspire them to work on tasks or movements in which they believe.
- Inspire them to develop their inner world.
- Show an interest in their feelings.
- Express your love for them, and not just their achievements.

Type Fours

What Does Love and Happiness Mean for This Type?

Fours are emotional and romantic and want to connect deeply and keep communicating. They tend to romanticize and idealize their partners, and sometimes this can mean they could have less realistic expectations in a relationship.

They literally would love riding off into the sunset with you.

What Attracts a Type Four?

They want you to be as focused on the relationship as they are. Partners who can share authentically and openly, and who can express their own emotions clearly and well are very attractive to them. If you can enter a growth journey with them, you might have their hearts for life.

Do:

- Welcome their creativity, receptivity, and depth of feeling.
- Accept their feelings and mood swings and honestly talk about how this affects you.
- Show your love as often as possible. Find out their love language to know whether this would be through gifts of quality time, service, words, or presents.
- When they are frustrated, don't rush in with easy solutions, it is more important for them to get your sympathy, understanding, and acceptance.
- Understand their needs to experience and express their feelings.
- Create a safe atmosphere for them to express their intense emotions.
- Encourage them to enjoy the present, engage in creativity, and show their works to others.

Type Fives

What Does Love and Happiness Mean for This Type?

They long for a partner who is patient and supportive, and who also gives them plenty of space to think.

What Attracts Type Five:

An independent partner who connects with them but also knows when to give them space and time to themselves. Someone who has their own interests, friends, and hobbies and can entertain themselves to a large degree is ideal.

Do:

- Praise their objectivity, intelligence, and a keen mind.
- Communicate clearly and directly.
- Let them know that you value their wise advice.
- Tell them what you want in a neutral tone, as if simply stating a fact.
- Respect their need for privacy when they work on their projects and ideas.
- Maintain a harmonious home atmosphere in which there are no surprises.
- If you want to do something new, give them plenty of time to think about this idea - with no pressure.
- Pinpoint the problems you are having, and set aside special, limited time to discuss them.
- When discussing problems, avoid dramatics. Stay calm.

Type Sixes

What Does Love and Happiness Mean for This Type?

It means being able to trust and feel safe with their partner.

What Attracts a Type Six?

They love free-spirited idealists. No matter what, their partner needs to help keep them focused on the positive aspects of life.

Do:

- Appreciate their loyalty, intelligence, empathy, and a keen mind.
- Appreciate their ability to anticipate dangers and deal with critical situations.
- Be open and honest. They feel more secure when all the cards are on the table. Let all your agreements be clear and clear so that there are no reasons for doubt.
- Do not beat around the bush or try to be clever and manipulative with them.
- In a conflict situation, show them that you are looking for a way to solve it constructively.
- If they start to rage, you need to step aside and let them freely pour out their anger. Your retaliatory aggression or fear will only add fuel to the fire.
- Encourage them to talk about their fears.
- If their fears begin to drive you crazy, be honest with them.
- Encourage them to exercise. Exercise prevents and alleviates anxiety and stress.
- Inspire them in certain situations to stop thinking and take action.

- Show them that some situations involve moderate risk, and that's still ok.
- Focus their attention on the best that can happen, and not on the worst.
- Encourage them to learn to trust their own decisions.

Type Sevens

What Does Love and Happiness Mean for This Type?

Adventure, fun, and sunshine. They want passion, enthusiasm for life, and all that it holds.

What Attracts a Type Seven?

Variety, excitement, and adventure. Someone interesting, light-hearted and engaged with many activities, friends and hobbies of their own, who will pay them attention and go along with their adventures too.

Do:

- Welcome their optimism, spontaneity, and enthusiasm.
- Listen to their stories, participate with them in fascinating conversations, adventures, and entertainment.
- Avoid too many rules and routines.
- Develop your own hobbies and interests so that you are interested in your own right.
- Inspire them to do regular exercise.
- Help them find ways to deal with and endure the less pleasant or dull parts of life.
- Encourage them to experience the full range of emotions: joy and pain, pleasure, and sorrow.

Type Eights

What Does Love and Happiness Mean for This Type?

Eights need relationships that connect, while still allowing independence. They like to protect and serve.

What Attracts Type Eight:

A partner who is prepared to follow rather than lead. Someone who can respect them and support them while still being an independent being. Honest and open communication.

Do:

- Express gratitude for their strength, self-confidence, and sense of justice.
- Be honest and direct with them.
- Let them know if they hurt you. They may not be aware of the effects of their actions.
- Set healthy boundaries.
- Stand up for yourself - do not let them push you around or ignore your point of view.
- Work out compromises together that will allow both to maintain self-esteem. Go for win-win results.
- Give them space and time to cool down if they get angry or aggressive.
- Respect their need to be alone from time to time.
- Inspire them to relax and exercise regularly.
- Help them feel comfortable when they talk about their problems and share their vulnerability with you.

Type Nines

What Does Love and Happiness Mean for This Type?

Nines love supportive, encouraging relationships with people who will work with them to achieve happiness.

What Attracts Type Nine?

A person who will be patient and encouraging. Someone who will attempt to understand them.

Do:

- Express gratitude for their kindness and patience.
- Shower them with physical and verbal affection and support.
- Be quick with thanks and slow with criticism and reproaches.
- Be patient.
- Give them enough time to decide.
- Use caution when you need to criticize or ask them to do something. They will accept requests expressed as "Could you do ...?" or "Will you help me, please?"
- Ignore their grunts and complaints when under pressure. Don't take it too personally.
- Invite them to openly express their dissatisfaction.
- Help them maintain a harmonious, peaceful atmosphere all around.
- Gently motivate them to prioritize and set goals.

Chapter 8: Enneagram in Your Business

Figuring out that difficult boss or demotivated team members using Enneagram may be the key to a calm and productive work environment. If you can harness your team's strengths and remain aware of the potential difficulties, it can really make your workdays a much more pleasant experience.

Part 1: Creating a Dream Team

Getting the right combination of people and skills really helps the wheels turn.

If we separate the activities of an organization or team into four main components, they might look like this:

P (Producing) - creating the widgets, providing the services, meeting the deadlines, and completing the tasks.

A (Administrating) - the supportive administrative tasks that enable the production to happen.

E (Entrepreneurial) - creating a vision and seeing opportunities, implementing changes.

I (Integrating) - The ability to pull all the other roles together with communication, management, and mediation, to form a cohesive whole.

Teams need elements of all the four components to be truly effective.

Our Enneatypes directly affect which roles we will fit into best, which tasks would suit us, and with what situations we would need the most support.

Your Enneatype determines which roles you perform brilliantly, which you would be good at, and in which you cannot cope at all.

The main characteristics of people predisposed to different roles are summarized in the table below and linked to their Enneatype.

P (Producing)	A (Administrative)	E (Entrepreneurial)	I (Integrating)
Results-oriented Pragmatic Hardworking Productive Impatient Competent	Pays attention to detail Organized Systems-thinker Problem-solver Methodical Conservative Loves spreadsheets, systems, clear guidelines, and numbers.	Dreamer Innovator Enthusiastic Inspirational Creative Not afraid of change Charismatic Needs freedom of thought and action.	Good listeners Able to create an atmosphere of mutual respect and trust. Great at managing conflict. Reasonable Fair Supportive
Excellent 3, 8	Excellent 6, 1	Excellent 5, 7, 8	Excellent 2, 9, 4
Good 1, 5, 2, 4, 6, 9	Good 3, 9	Good 4	Good 1, 6, 7
Tend to be Weak 7	Tend to be Weak 2, 4, 7, 8, 5	Tend to be Weak 1, 9, 6	Tend to be Weak 3, 5, 8

When balancing a team - it is important to remember that people cannot play several roles at the same time and remain effective in all of them. Certain types are diametrically opposed, so someone who is a great administrator may battle to take risks and be entrepreneurial, for example.

So, choosing your dream team - if you are that lucky to be able to - or task reallocation - may be key to maximum performance.

To decide how best to combine your team - it may help to consider the primary function of the team, the end goals, or take a more balanced approach and ensure that you put Enneatypes in roles that match their strengths.

However, you choose to do it, you can improve the current situation by:

1. Analyzing and checking everyone's Enneatype.
2. Looking at the role and tasks they are currently required to perform.
3. Considering how to shift, alter, or reallocate tasks to team members who are better suited or stronger in these areas.
4. Or, if the above is not possible, to mentor and support an individual with:
    a. An assigned assistant or mentor who can bolster their weak areas
    b. Growth tasks to move the Enneatype towards a higher level of development within their type

You wouldn't ask a fish to climb a tree, so insisting a person perform a task which is obviously not a strength is not only putting them under unreasonable pressure, but also putting you under strain in continual and increased management needs, and taking up extra resources too.

People perform faster, are more productive, motivated, and happier when they can focus where their strengths lie.

Part 2: Working with the Types

In general - each type responds best when you approach tasks in a certain way with them.

1st Enneatype

Question-motivation for the task: Ask them how to correctly, accurately, and timeously complete the task.

Advice to the leader: The best way to motivate a One is to entrust them with something to correct or improve. The tasks should be formulated as concretely and in as much detail as possible, with clear terms and criteria for evaluating the result. A One can appear critical and hard - when they are really focused on the task.

Always speak constructively and to the point.

2nd Enneatype

Question-motivation for the task: Ask them how they can help and what kind of support they can provide someone.

Advice to the leader: It is important to establish warm, friendly contact with people of this nature. From time to time, you will need to express your appreciation and gratitude for the tasks and assignments completed and show how much you value them.

3rd Enneatype

Question-motivation for the task: What do you need to do to succeed?

Advice to the leader: Clearly state the purpose of the assignment. Describe the rewards and successes that await them as a result of achieving the goal. People of this type are well motivated by public praise and recognition of their merits. Never criticize them in the presence of strangers. Help them save face and bolster their public image.

4th Enneatype

Question-motivation for the task: Ask them how to make it unique.

Advice to the leader: It is important to establish personal contact with Fours. Let them express their emotions, listen to them, and be sincere with them. Leave space for creativity in tasks. It is important that your criticism concerns a specific task, and not the employee himself and his personal qualities.

5th Enneatype

Question motivation for the task: What information is needed?

Advice to the leader: When formulating the task, be specific and logical. Allow enough time for reflection and research. Keep things calm and unemotional. The best motivation for Fives is the ability to work autonomously, independently carrying out a project from start to finish.

6th Enneatype

Question-motivation for completing a task: What is the worst-case scenario?

Advice to the leader: Communicate with them on an equal footing. When proposing a new project, it is better to be upfront about how everyone will benefit (including yourself) and discuss possible difficulties and contingencies. Calmly relate your doubts and challenges. Humor is a great way to ease conversations here.

7th Enneatype

Question-motivation for the task: What else can be done?

Advice to the leader: Be positive and maintain an atmosphere of optimism. Refer to new opportunities and prospects. It is best to use the potential of such an employee in creative projects and communicate with them on an equal footing. Give clear time frames and consequences of missed deadlines.

8th Enneatype

Question-motivation for the task: Who is responsible, and what are we fighting for?

Advice to the leader: Eights need to know that you are a strong leader, and you will take responsibility for your words and actions. Communicate with them sincerely, openly, and authentically. Express confidence in them and have a results-centered approach. Check in at milestones to ensure everything is on track.

9th Enneatype

Question-motivation for the task: How to maintain a state of comfort, stability, and have everyone's opinion heard?

Advice to the leader: When setting tasks, explain to them the situation, without going into too much detail. Make it clear that you value their work and listen to their opinion. Maintain a positive, harmonious atmosphere in the team.

The Building, Maintaining and Motivating Your Team - a Quick Reference

Use this information as a quick reference guide when recruiting, managing, distributing tasks, developing, and promoting each type.

<u>Type Ones</u>
What motivates them?
Social justice.
A mission or values-based goal.
Fairness.
Finding solutions.
Pursuing personal growth.
Respect and airtime for their ideas.
Something to correct or improve.

What demotivates them?
Criticism from those they admire.
Feeling like they can't make a difference.
Corruption, unethical choices, unfairness, gray areas.
When people don't follow specific instructions.
Being labelled as too critical or meticulous.
Inefficiency and inaccuracy.

How to Communicate Best?

Take them seriously.
Keep to times and schedules.
Be clear.
Be concise.
Encourage them to share their thoughts.

How to resolve conflict?

Be clear.
Be fair.
Admit your own mistakes.
Allow them to reflect.

How to Help Them Grow?

Teach them how to use mistakes as growth tools.
Show them how to be more flexible.
Give feedback gently and be specific.
Ask for their thoughts and solutions.
Show them how to correct others more constructively.

Type Twos

What motivates them?

Feeling welcome and cared about.
Being able to help and serve others.
Meeting goals.
Real appreciation.
Affirmation of their value.
Someone doing a good deed for them without being asked.

What demotivates them?

They burnout easily if left to their own devices - get them to take breaks and practice self-care.
Criticism and neglect.

Being overwhelmed by too many needs or tasks.

How to Communicate Best?

Be attentive, supportive, and encouraging.
Listen.
Allow time for polite or casual conversation.
Encourage their participation in the conversation.

How to resolve conflict?

Be gentle.
Be inclusive.
Share thoughts and feelings and listen to their side too.
Remind them of their value.
Focus on the problem, not the person.

How to Help Them Grow?

Teach them to accept help.
Addressing problems.
Self-care.
Recognize their contribution before sharing concerns.

<u>**Type Threes**</u>

What motivates them?

Completing tasks and goals.
Acceptance and appreciation.
Fresh, new goals, challenges and responsibilities.
Meeting new people.
Public events.

What demotivates them?

Repetitive failure - especially in the same task or area.
Negative perceptions of others.
Emotional conflicts.

Being ignored or frequently criticized.
Failure to give them credit for achievements.
Disrespect or open dislike of others.

How to Communicate Best?

Be clear, concise and specific.
Be straightforward.
Help them understand what you require of them.

How to resolve conflict?

Use constructive criticism.
Share your feelings and let them share theirs.
Help them feel valued.
Focus on the problem, not the person.

How to Help Them Grow?

Show them what they have already achieved and what they must be grateful about.
Showing blind spots.
Showing their value is more than their achievements.

<u>**Type Fours**</u>

What motivates them?

Building connections.
Lots of personal time.
The ability to express their emotions through some form of art or creative task.
Feeling accepted and valued.
When people share or understand their vision.

What demotivates them?

Meaningless chit-chat.
Large groups.

Routine and dullness.
Rigid environments which don't allow creativity.
Interruptions.
Unresolved conflicts.

How to Communicate Best?

Avoid too much logic.
Focus on feelings and connections.
Optimism.
Be encouraging.
Be authentic and expressive.

How to resolve conflict?

Openly share thoughts and feelings.
Brainstorm with them.
Empathize.

How to Help Them Grow?

Taking time to reflect on what is working or not working.
Allowing others to help them.
Recognizing others' needs.
Managing stress.

Type Fives

What motivates them?

New discoveries.
Time alone.
New skills or techniques.
Being valued and appreciated for their abilities.

What demotivates them?

Large groups.
Emotional overload or situations.

Serving others.
Lack of peace.

How to Communicate Best?

Allow space and time to reflect.
Be clear and logical.
Avoid drama and emotions.
Skip small talk.

How to resolve conflict?

Be honest about problems.
Troubleshoot and brainstorm constructive solutions.
Be logical.
Look at both sides.

How to Help Them Grow?

Listening skills.
Connecting to their emotions.
Connecting to others.

Type Sixes

What motivates them?

Being given responsibility.
Consistency.
Trust.
Helping others.
Deep connections.

What demotivates them?

Inconsistency.
Unreliability.
Insecurity about the future.
Feeling unwanted or unneeded.

Failure.

How to Communicate Best?

Listen and offer support.
Encourage them.
Be direct and practical.

How to resolve conflict?

Be calm and logical.
Share your point of view.
Encourage them to express themselves.

How to Help Them Grow?

Creating boundaries.
Respect for others.
Future planning rather than fear.
Show how failure can create positive learning.

<u>Type Sevens</u>

What motivates them?

New ideas and experiences.
Creative outlets.
Lots of options and flexibility.
Connecting with people.

What demotivates them?

Isolation
Routine
Rigidity
Schedules
Lack of choices or freedom.

How to Communicate Best?

Be upbeat and positive.
Listen to them.
Appreciate their ideas.
Be clear.
Take a bit longer and include some casual conversation.

How to resolve conflict?

Be supportive and encouraging.
Be honest.
Encourage them to express themselves.
Brainstorm solutions together.

How to Help Them Grow?

Planning.
Completing tasks.
Working through negative emotions.
Mindfulness and calm.

<u>Type Eights</u>

What motivates them?

Leading and taking charge.
Making hard decisions.
Physical activity.
Practicality.
Respect.
Freedom.

What demotivates them?

Control.
Emotional situations.
Blame.
Dishonesty.
Out-of-control situations.

How to Communicate Best?

Be direct.
Be open to their ideas.
Be logical and practical.
Be clear and concise.

How to resolve conflict?

Brainstorm solutions together.
Be respectful and solution-focused.
Share, but be clear on boundaries.

How to Help Them Grow?

Listening and empathy.
Allowing others, a turn.
Being vulnerable.
Sharing and expressing themselves.

<u>Type Nines</u>

What motivates them?

Stability.
Consistency.
Mediating problems between groups.
Safety and acceptance.
Being heard.

What demotivates them?

Being put under pressure or given hard choices.
Interruption.
Being ignored.
Unresolved conflicts.

How to Communicate Best?

Allow for small-talk and personal connection.
Be clear.

How to resolve conflict?

Create a safe space.
Avoid pressure.
Encourage sharing of emotions and ideas.
Avoid negativity or criticism.
Stay calm.

How to Help Them Grow?

Conflict-handling skills.
Facing challenges. Acting.

Chapter 9: Enneagram Tests

Finally, we come to the interesting part. You may have even skipped ahead to this chapter, just to find out what your type is, and what your partner, children, friends, and coworkers' types are.

This is the fun part - because we may think we know our types, or then again, we may be a bit confused, seeing a bit of every type in ourselves.

There are some quick and easy tests you can use to help you with this.

Enneatype Test One - Quick Test

In each section, pick the one paragraph that most accurately describes you, in your opinion. Consider how you are at this point of your life - not thinking too much about the past or about how you would like to be. Be honest with yourself.

Having made a choice, do not re-analyze it.

Once you've chosen the paragraph, write down the letter of that paragraph title. Then go look at the test key.Choose one of these:

A. Confident

I consider myself a very independent and confident person. I am convinced that life is better if you boldly face it. I set goals and do everything necessary to achieve them. I do not want a simple existence; I want to achieve something great and make a significant contribution to the lives of people around me. I do not seek out conflict, but I do not allow people to put pressure on me either. Most of the time, I know exactly what I want, and move in that direction.

I like to work hard and enjoy life to the fullest.

B. Executive

It is important for me to be busy. I am responsible and faithful. I feel terrible if I cannot fulfill my obligations or do what others expect of me. I want people to know how much I care about them. I try to do everything for their benefit. I often make some do things for the well-being of others, and it doesn't matter whether they know about it or not. I am sometimes unable to take good care of myself. I work when I need to, and I relax or do something pleasant only in my free time.

C. Closed

I tend to be quiet and spend a lot of time alone. I like to reflect and remember. Social activity is not very important to me, and in general, it is unusual for me to take an especially energetic part in public life. I don't really like to lead people or live in a state of constant competition. Many will call me a dreamer. I like calm and quiet. I don't need constant movement and achievement.

Now write down A, B, or C - depending on which paragraph you believe describes you best.

Next, you will choose your second letter from one of the following paragraphs.

P. Positive

I am a person with a positive outlook and am convinced that everything in life is happening as it should. I always find new sources of inspiration and enthusiastically accept new opportunities and projects. I like to communicate with people and help them become happier. I like to share my joy and well-being with others. (Of course, I do not always feel good, but I try not to show it to anyone!) It seems to me that my eternal cheerfulness relates to my unwillingness to delve into myself for a long time and sort out my own problems.

S. Sensual/Expressive

I am a person with strong feelings and emotions. People can easily see when I'm upset about something. I try to be more careful with people, but still, I can't restrain my strong emotions around them. I like it when I clearly know where I stand and what I can rely on. In the same way, I always let others understand how I feel about them. When I'm upset with something, I like to see that those around me sympathize and empathize with me. Although I know the "rules of the game," I don't like it when someone tells me what to do. I like to make decisions on my own.

L. Logical/Competent

I try to be logical and restrained. I'm uncomfortable dealing with strong emotions. In my work, I strive for the best, almost perfect results. I prefer to do everything myself. In conflict situations, I try not to show my own feelings. People see me as cold and aloof. I do not want my emotional reactions to interfere with important business. I also do not show any feelings if others are trying to get to me that way.

Now choose your second letter and write it next to your first one, so you will have something like AP or CS. Use the test key to see what Enneatype might be dominant for you.

Test Key

BL – 1 type

BP – 2 type

AL – 3 type

CS – 4 type

CL – 5 type

BS – 6 type

AP – 7 type

AS – 8 type

CP – 9 type

Enneatype Test Two - In-depth Test

If you felt Test One wasn't close enough, then this test will help you can determine your type of Enneagram with greater accuracy. When observing other people, you can also use these questions to help you determine their type.

How to Calculate Your Results

On a piece of paper, create nine columns and label each from one through to nine. As you answer each question, put a tick or check mark in the corresponding column.

For example - if you said your torso is an hourglass shape - you would place a tick in columns three and four. Pick only one answer for each question.

At the end of the questionnaire, one of the types will have the most check marks, and this will then be your dominant type. The others will be complementary.

Section 1: Appearance

1. Describe your overall torso shape

Hourglass - 3, 4

Rectangular - 1, 2, 5, 6, 8

Oval - 9

Circle - 7

Square - 5

Triangle base down (or pear-shaped) - 4

Triangle base up – 2

2. Are you inclined to be overweight?

Yes, but I can change it if I wish and strengthen it - 3, 4, 9

No, and never was - 1, 2, 8

No, but it can vary - 3, 6, 9

3. Your height

Up to 155cm/5' – 1, 2

From 155cm to 165cm/5' to 5'5" –1, 2, 5, 6

From 165cm to 175cm/5'5" to 5'9" – 1, 2, 3, 4, 5, 6, 7

175cm to 185cm/5'9" to 6' – 3, 7, 8, 9

From 185cm and above/over 6' - 3, 8, 9

4. Describe your face shape

Oval - 3, 4, 9

Circle - 7

Triangle - 1, 2, 6

Square - 5

Rectangle – 8

5. How do you usually dress?

Discreetly, so as not to attract excessive attention - 1, 6

Bright, to stand out from the crowd - 2, 3, 4, 7

According to the situation and the necessary impression - 2, 3, 8

Convenient and practically - 4, 5, 8, 9

Unusual and extravagant - 2, 4, 7

Section 2: Behavior

1. Your speech is usually

Restrained, laconic, without unnecessary emotions - 1, 5, 6, 8, 9

Emotional, and quick - 2, 3, 7,

Calm and measured - 4, 6, 9

It has an indicative character - 3, 5, 8

2. How would you describe your communication with people?

Forced - 1

Easy and laid back - 2, 3, 4,

Patronizing - 7, 8

According to need - 5, 6

Energizing - 2, 3, 4

3. How do you feel about loneliness?

I need it like the air - 1, 5, 9

I cannot stand it - 2, 3, 7

Calm - 4, 6, 8

I see no reason to be lonely - 2, 3, 7, 8,

4. In a relationship, you usually play the role of?

Assistant - 2, 4

Faithful friend - 1, 4, 6

Patron - 7, 8

Leader - 3, 7, 8

The second half - 1, 2, 4

Inspirational muse - 3, 4, 6,

5. Do you help other people?

Yes, I always see what another person needs - 2, 4, 8

No, I think that everyone should take care of themselves - 1, 3, 5

Yes, and often I forget about myself, helping others - 2, 4, 9,

Yes, but only if necessary and possible - 6, 9

I help and patronize people close to me - 7, 8,

6. Do you meet new people easily?

Yes, for me it is very simple - 2, 3, 4, 7

Outwardly easy, but internally I keep my distance - 6, 9

No, it takes a long time - 1, 5, 6

Yes, if it meets my goals - 8

No, you can't trust people you don't know well - 1, 5

7. What is most important for you in a person?

Status and position in society - 2, 3, 7

Abilities - 1, 7, 8

Honesty and integrity - 5

Consciousness and humanity - 4

Usefulness - 1, 2, 6, 8

Unobtrusiveness and calm - 1, 9

Inner light - 4

8. How do you usually solve problems?

I think that 99% of problems are solved by themselves - 9, 7

I have many options for quickly resolving the issue - 2

I make a balanced decision - 1, 5, 6

I act decisively and assertively - 8

I find someone who can decide this - 6

I'm experiencing and looking for support - 4

I don't notice them - 7, 9

Section Three: Your perception of the world

1. What would define how your credo?

There is no limit to perfection (1)

Impossible is possible (2)

An external impression is the key to success (3)

Whatever is done is all for the better (4)

Life is a struggle (5)

Life is an obstacle course (6)

Life should be fun; only then does it make sense (7)

I know what this world should be like (8)

The main thing is not to run out of breath at the very beginning (9)

It is only necessary to do what brings happiness (7)

2. How would you classify yourself?

Optimist - 2, 3, 4, 7

Pessimist - 1, 5, 9

Realist - 6, 8

Section Four: Thinking

Which statements do you agree with unconditionally?

I am almost never satisfied with my results. I think that you can always do better (1).

The main thing is not the form but the essence (1).

In order to feel better, I need privacy and order (1).

It often seems to me that other people are too slow in movements, thoughts, feelings (2).

I like the praise and approval of my actions and qualities (2).

I always have a lot of options on how to solve a question (2).

I am devoted to myself. For me, being sincere and real is much more important than being comfortable (2).

The most important thing in society is to present yourself properly (3).

I love and know how to be in the spotlight (3).

I choose only the best (3).

I am equally kind to everyone around me (4).

Helping others, I kind of find the meaning of life (4).

I often imagine myself as someone else, experiencing their feelings, suffering, and events (4).

Better slowly but surely (5).

I trust only serious, thoughtful, thoughtful people (5).

I am a straightforward and honest person (5).

I always try to make rules in everything (6).

I have strong self-control (6).

I always try to foresee undesirable consequences (6).

Life is given for pleasure, and tomorrow may not come (7).

I know my worth. It is uniquely high (7).

Any problem is simply a poorly chosen point of view (7).

It is only necessary to do what brings happiness (7).

I really see the miraculous in the ordinary (7).

I like to have fun and mix with a bright circle of people (7).

I am a person of work. The main thing is that things move forward (8).

I strive to effectively organize people around me (8).

I remove barriers to the goal without regret (8).

Everyone has the right to their opinion (9).

I always look at the situation from the side (9).

Life should be measured and take its course (9).

Adding it all up

You will now have a lot of numbers appearing on your notepad under each type. Which type has the most ticks or check marks?

Go back to Chapter Two and read up again about your dominant type. Ask yourself how much you can learn now that you have more insight into yourself.

Chapter 10: Using the Enneagram in Everyday Life

In Personal Development

Creating self-awareness is always a slightly painful process. Once we have a handle on our Enneatype, we might feel like rejecting elements of it. Some of the weaknesses may feel a bit threatening or not like us at all.

Take some time to reflect on how the Enneatype might show you parts of yourself, which may need some attention. Let's call them blind spots. Open yourself up to the possibility that these things might, at times, be true for you.

Also, celebrate your strengths.

Knowing the whole of yourself, you now can see where you can better use your strengths - in your relationship, family, or at work.

And you can quietly start working on your weaknesses, starting with an awareness of when and where you might be acting them out.

More importantly, you will now know how to grow further, and what Enneatype you revert to under stress or in good times. You may also get a sense of the level of your development and how much further you need to go to be the best you can be.

In Interacting with the World

The more you become familiar with the various Enneatypes, the more you will find yourself looking at people and really seeing them. You will see their outward, maybe less useful behavior patterns and say, "Aha, I get what is really going on. I understand your fears and dislikes. Your deep desires and your goals."

You will get an insight that provides the ability for patience, kindness, and understanding of others. Because now you see past the behavior to the real person beneath it. And now you realize there is hope for everyone. That we are all truly different, and that in our diversity lies our strength. We all bring different abilities to the party, making for one well-rounded, rich tapestry of life.

As you learn about each type, you climb inside their world, get how they might feel and why they do the things they do.

You can then choose your responses based on your new knowledge of yourself and of them - hopefully, with better outcomes for everyone.

What an incredible power to have!

In the Family and Relationships

Ah, those first moments of a new passion, when nothing your new love does, is wrong. When you are giddy with excitement and flushed with love chemicals.

What a rush!

It is so difficult to see past all this to whom the person truly is.

And when the hormones and the rush wear off, we are left looking at a person who we don't really understand, and perhaps don't like as much as we thought.

If only we could get past this challenge - we might avoid the huge and growing number of divorces, broken hearts, and broken families.

We could understand each other a little more, and perhaps even have the insight to see each other more clearly from the beginning. Maybe we could make more informed choices in the full knowledge of what and who it was we were signing up for. Maybe we could adjust our expectations slightly, to accommodate our own type, and our growth and that of our partner.

Whether you are in the first flush of love or feel you have given too much already and it's over, with your new knowledge, you have a chance to step back and review the situation.

And even if you throw your current relationship in the trash, be aware that until you understand your patterns and choices, you are doomed to repeat them. So now would the time to stop and analyze what these might be and how they influence your choice of partner and how each relationship unfolds.

In Business

Much as we choose our romantic partners, we enter a new work environment and a new set of colleagues full of hope.

A person's professional characteristics, and what appears on their resume or CV, is so much less than what we really need to know about them.

Will we be a good fit for the new boss or recruit?

Should we go into a partnership with this person?

Are we even in the right kind of job?

How good will our new employee really be? Will they be able to meet the demands of the position?

And that problematic colleague. What is really going on there?

Thanks to the use of the Enneagram, you will have a much better insight and improve your chances of answering any of these questions.

If your team isn't producing at the level you would like, or it has become toxic and unpleasant - look to the Enneagram for help.

You will also know how best to use the people's resources at your disposal.

You need a new injection of vision and some new ideas - get some Twos and Fours to help you out. A Two will have the ideas, and a Four will know which ones might succeed.

Then get a One to critically evaluate the plan for loopholes and practicality, and help you structure milestones and find any gaps.

Next, ask a Five or a Six to look for weaknesses and contingencies. A Three to help you bring the project to fruition and an Eight to help the One with the project plan and next step, perhaps even the strategic vision.

Put them all in a think tank for a truly stupendous strategy and business success.

And then, allocate tasks to the right types. Don't ask a Seven to manage your production line, and don't stick a Two or a Four into the clerks' corner. Whatever you do, don't leave an Eight or a Three to keep your team happy and well-managed.

These are important things to know and apply for business success.

Conclusion

With awareness comes a little pain. Growth is never painless, and we often only do it when we become so uncomfortable with the present state of affairs that we simply must shift and change to find some ease and release of pressure.

While it feels hard in the moment, in the end, we can heave a sigh of relief. We can look back and realize how far we have come and how much better life is now.

By being open to some discomfort, we create an incredible space for ourselves to grow into and become more than we were before.

What is so apparent is that no Enneatype is better or worse than any other. What they all have in common is a foundation of experiences that created faulty thinking and some overtly useful but long-term very limiting patterns.

Only by identifying what these might be, do we have any hope of keeping the good stuff and shifting the things which are no longer useful in our lives.

What is also true is that everybody alive has an Enneatype, wherever they may sit on their level of development it took some doing to get from basic instinct through to more helpful and useful choices and a happier life.

Every single person alive has had a childhood in which various challenges shaped them into what they have now become. This doesn't mean that they necessarily had bad childhoods or were worse off than anyone else. No matter what you do, you cannot raise a child in perfect isolation from any sort of challenge. In some sort of glass jar like a science experiment.

Growth means change, and it means challenges. With each challenge or event, we learn something new, a new pattern of coping and surviving. Sometimes these lessons are useful, and sometimes they are destructive. And depending on how we experience each challenge or what idea we have about it, we create a new pattern of behavior.

Things will happen, and each event - even if it may appear innocuous to an outsider - has the potential to shape the child's character one way or another. What is experienced as very traumatic for one person may not be a problem for another.

Our brains are the most incredible survival machines. They will take reality and shape it in such a way that it makes life easier. If that means altering reality, distorting facts, or creating what to the outside may look like self-destructive behavior, our brains only care is that the result helps us to survive - mentally, emotionally, and physically - at that moment.

When new input comes along, we don't always change our survival patterns so easily. It takes a critical mass of new input, or great discomfort, to make us question what we think we know.

This is where the study of the Enneagram is so useful. Because unlike animals, we aren't just ruled by instinct and behavioral programming. We also can engage higher thinking to create new realities for ourselves.

Only by applying your newly acquired knowledge in practice, will you get really experienced at recognizing Enneagram types and selecting an individual approach to each type.

Never stop in your development and learning. Life is a journey of mountains, dragons, muddy swamps, gorgeous meadows and calm seas - these ups and downs we travel to become our highest and most fulfilled selves.

Utilizing Enneagram types in your life is like carrying a trusty map to navigate your adventures. I hope that the information in this book helps you on your path.

References

Enneagram of Personality. (2020, February 13). Retrieved from https://en.wikipedia.org/wiki/Enneagram_of_Personality

Fictional Types. (n.d.). Retrieved from http://davesenneagram.com/section/fictional-types

How the System Works. (n.d.). Retrieved from https://www.enneagraminstitute.com/how-the-enneagram-system-works

Phifer-Ritchie, R. (2019, April 1). Enneagram Jokes - The Lighter Side of Type - How Many... Retrieved from https://www.relationshipdoctoronline.com/on-the-lighter-side-of-type/

Ross, Venkatraman, R., & Horvath, C. (2014, May 30). "Harry Potter" and the nine personality types. Retrieved from https://www.mugglenet.com/2014/05/harry-potter-and-the-9-personality-types

The app that tells you anyone's personality. (n.d.). Retrieved from https://www.crystalknows.com/

The Nine Enneagram Types. (n.d.). Retrieved from https://theenneagramatwork.com/nine-enneagram-types

WHAT IS THE ENNEAGRAM? | The Simple Beginners Guide - YouTube. (n.d.). Retrieved from https://www.youtube.com/watch?v=Mdc2PMAvpqw